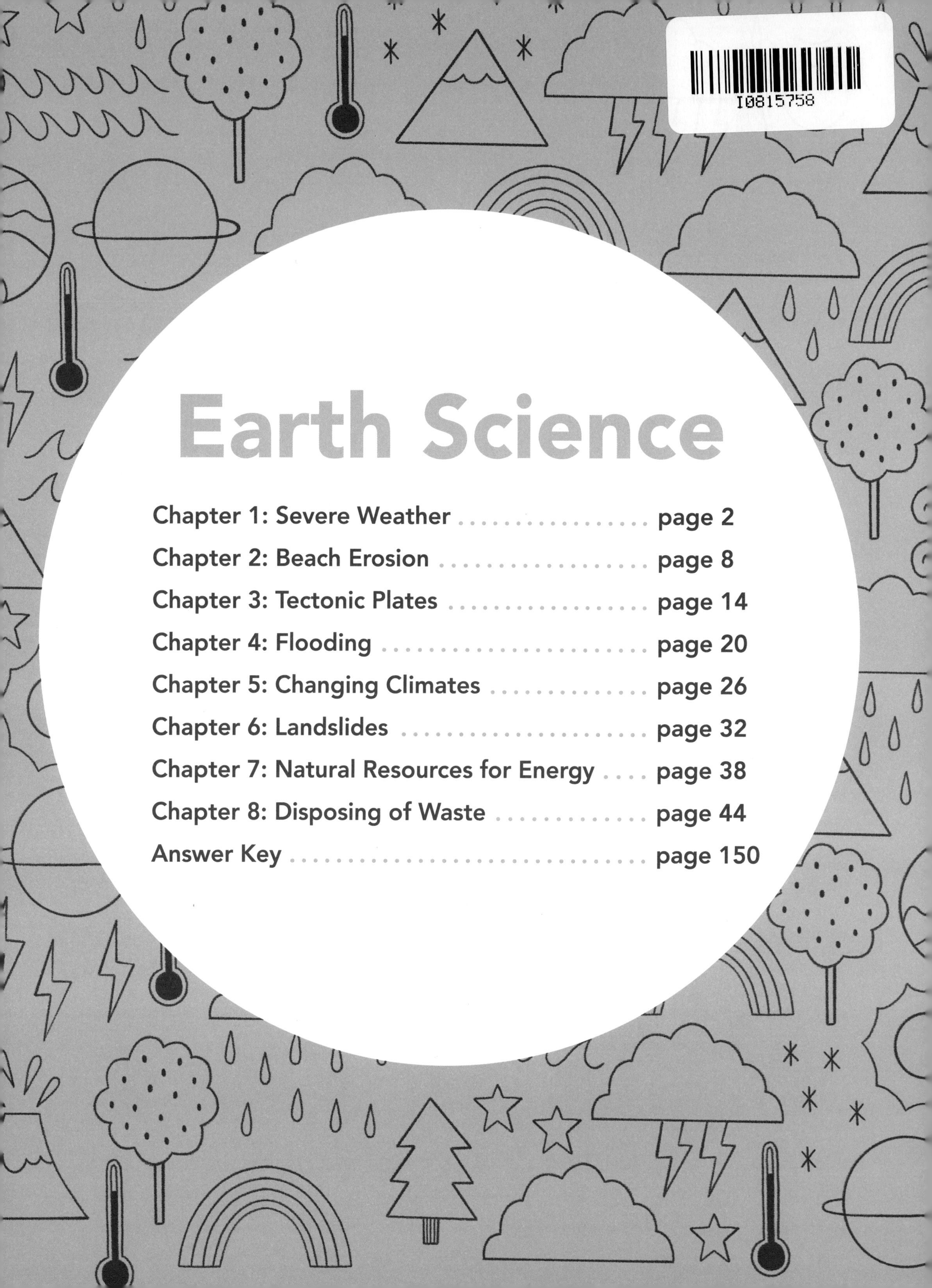

Earth Science

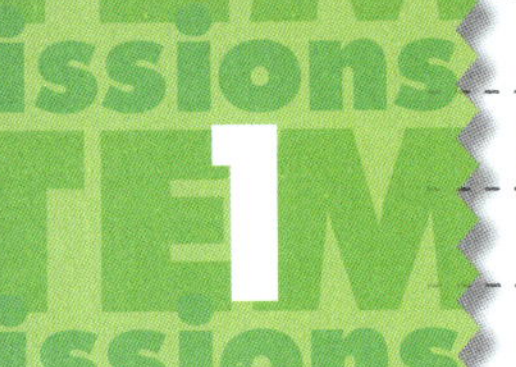

Chapter 1

Severe Weather

What is weather? Where does weather come from?

 Read the key points. When you finish, check the box.

Key Points: What is weather?

When you wake up in the morning, before you start to get ready for the day, you probably look outside to check the weather. You need to know if it is raining or sunny and if it will be hot or cold. Knowing the weather will help you prepare for the day.

But what exactly is weather? **Weather** is a combination of short-term events that happen each day in the layer of gas surrounding the earth, called the **atmosphere**. Weather is different in different parts of the world and it changes over minutes, hours, days, or weeks. These changes are caused by factors such as temperature and winds.

You may already know that weather can refer to the temperature outside, the amount of sunlight, and the amount of precipitation such as rain or snow in an area. But, weather can also include factors such as wind speed; how much moisture is in the air, or its humidity; and atmospheric pressure, or the force produced by the gases surrounding the earth.

 Complete the exercise.

Test your knowledge

(1) Which best describes weather?

A. We can only learn the weather by watching TV.
B. Weather is a combination of short-term events that happen each day in our atmosphere.
C. Weather is the same every day, and is not affected by temperature and wind.

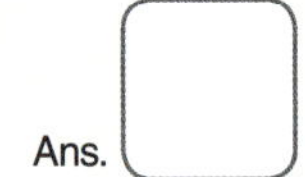

Ans.

(2) Which is not a factor of weather?

A. amount of sunlight

B. precipitation

C. weight

D. wind speed

E. temperature

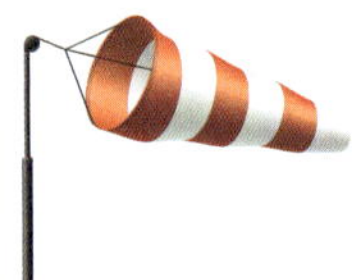

Ans.

2

Chapter 1
Severe Weather

What types of weather do you experience most days? Have you ever experienced severe weather?

Read the key points below. When you finish, check the box.

Key Points: Types of Severe Weather

In some cases, severe weather conditions can develop. **Severe weather** is any weather event that can threaten a community's safety or cause damage to people and property. Some examples of severe weather events can include heat waves, droughts, blizzards, and powerful hurricanes or cyclones.

One of the most common types of severe weather is a thunderstorm. Thunderstorms can cause weather events such as lightning, hail, strong winds, flooding and even tornadoes. If you live in an area where thunderstorms are common, you may have experienced some of these events.

Lightning: Lightning is the release of electricity that happens high in the atmosphere, or in-between the atmosphere and the ground. Lightning forms during severe thunderstorms from charged particles in the air. If lightning strikes the ground it can start fires and damage buildings.

Tornadoes: A tornado is a dangerous rotating column of air created by the strong winds of a thunderstorm. If a tornado gets large enough to reach the ground it can cause terrible damage to buildings, vehicles, trees, and anything else in its path.

Hail: Pieces of ice that fall from clouds during a severe thunderstorm are called hail. Hail can be different sizes, from a pebble to a golf ball or even the size of a softball! Large pieces of hail can be dangerous and cause damage to cars, buildings, and trees.

Strong winds: Thunderstorms can create winds up to 100 miles per hour! These winds can knock over trees and break windows.

Flash flooding: Flash flooding is also a concern during a severe thunderstorm. If a lot of rain falls quickly and the ground cannot absorb it, an area can flood quickly. Heavy rain is a common cause of flooding during a thunderstorm.

Complete the exercise.

Test your knowledge

Match the type of severe weather to the description. Choose the correct answer from the box below.

A: lightning B: hail C: tornado D. flash flooding

(1) A dangerous, rotating column of strong wind. Ans. ☐

(2) Pieces of ice that fall from a thunderstorm. Ans. ☐

(3) Electricity released from a thunderstorm created by charged particles in the air. Ans. ☐

(4) When heavy rain causes water to build up instead of being absorbed by the ground. Ans. ☐

3

Chapter 1

Severe Weather

Which type of warning system would be the best for alerting people to an incoming tornado?

Read the key points below. When you finish, check the box.

Key Points: Severe Weather Safety

When it comes to staying safe during severe weather events, like a thunderstorm, there are some solutions and safety measures available. For example, storm proof windows made with reinforced glass were created to help limit the damage caused by strong winds. In areas where hurricanes are more likely to happen, people sometimes put hurricane shutters on their houses to help decrease window damage. These inventions have proven to be effective for preventing damage to buildings.

While limiting the damage to buildings is important, scientists and engineers also focus on developing ways to keep people safe. This led to the development of warning systems that alert people to incoming dangerous storms so they can prepare or move somewhere safe. One example of this type of precaution is a siren warning system.

Siren warning systems can quickly send a message across a town or city to warn of possible danger. These systems produce a loud sound that informs people of a severe weather event. These systems were used as the primary alert method before TVs and phones were common. Sirens typically have a separate power source in case a storm causes the power to go out. This allows them to alert communities when phones and TVs don't work.

More recently, scientists and engineers have developed alert system that can be sent to cell phones to alert people of severe weather events. These alert messages are the quickest and most reliable way to inform people of possible severe weather events. Knowing about dangerous weather early on gives people and communities time to prepare and get to safety.

Complete the exercise.

Test your knowledge

Answer T for true or F for false.

(1) Hurricane shutters can reduce damage to windows.

Ans. [ ]

(2) The siren warning system does not work if power is lost due to severe weather.

Ans. [ ]

(3) Engineers are constantly working on solutions to protect us to people from severe weather.

Ans. [ ]

Chapter 1
Severe Weather

Use the word box below to fill in the blanks and review key vocabulary.

Review the Key Points

Weather is a combination of short-term events that happen each day in the layer of gas surrounding the earth, called the [ ]. Weather is different in different parts of the world and it changes over minutes, hours, days, or weeks. These changes are caused by factors such as temperature and winds.

You may already know that weather can refer to the temperature outside, the amount of sunlight, and the amount of precipitation such as rain or snow in an area. But, weather can also include factors such as wind speed; how much moisture is in the air, or its humidity; and atmospheric pressure, or the force produced by the gases surrounding the earth.

[ ] is any weather event that can threaten a community's safety or cause damage to people and property.

When it comes to staying safe during severe weather events, like a thunderstorm, there are some solutions and safety measures available. For example, storm proof windows made with reinforced glass were created to help limit the damage caused by strong winds. In areas where hurricanes are more likely to happen, people sometimes put hurricane [ ] on their houses to help decrease window damage.

While limiting the damage to buildings is important, scientists and engineers also focus on developing ways to keep people safe. This led to the development of warning systems that [ ] people to incoming dangerous storms so they can prepare or move somewhere safe. One example of this type of precaution is a siren warning system.

severe weather / atmosphere / alert / shutters

Complete the exercise.

Math Mission

Temperature can sometimes be an indicator that severe weather is likely to occur. Answer the following questions about the three thermometers on the right.

(1) What is the temperature indicated by thermometer A?

Ans. [ ] °F

(2) Find the difference between the temperatures indicated by thermometers B and C.

Ans. [ ] °F

(3) Find the difference between the highest and lowest temperatures.

Ans. [ ] °F

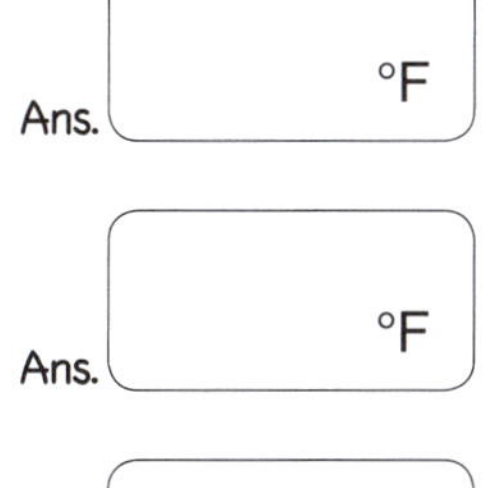

Chapter 1
Severe Weather

Read the mission. Then, answer the following questions to help you with your solution.

The Mission

Severe weather like thunderstorms, tornadoes, and hurricanes can cause terrible damage to buildings, homes, and communities. They can leave people without power, fresh water, food, or shelter. Design a system or a device that can protect a house from the dangerous effects of a thunderstorm.

Before you design...THINK!

1. Describe the mission in your own words.

2. Brainstorm about a solution. Write your notes in the space below. Use the following questions to guide your thinking:

(1) What type of prevention technology would you use?
(2) Can you improve on current devices? Or create a new solution?
(3) Can you create your own design to stop hail or tornado damage?

Chapter 1

Severe Weather

Read the mission. Then, draw and evaluate your solution.

The Mission

Design a system or a device that can protect a house from the dangerous effects of a thunderstorm.

Design

Draw or write about your solution below.

Evaluate

Evaluate your severe weather protection system. Do you think it would work? Did you choose to create a new device or improve an existing one?

Chapter 2 Beach Erosion

What is erosion?

 Read the key points. When you finish, check the box.

Key Points: Erosion and Weathering

Have you ever looked at the landscape around you and wondered if it looks the same as it did 1,000 years ago? The answer is no! The earth's features were shaped over many years by natural processes called weathering and erosion.

Weathering is the breaking down of rock and solid landforms into smaller pieces. **Erosion** is the process that transports the smaller pieces of rock, soil, and sand from one location to another. One of the main forces on Earth that causes erosion is water. Some other sources of erosion are wind, glacial, chemical, temperature, and human activities.

Water erosion is when pieces of rock, sand, or loose soil are carried or worn away by water.

Wind erosion is when wind moves loose rock, soil, and sand from one place to another.

Glacial erosion is when a slow moving mass of ice called a glacier moves across the land carrying away rock and soil.

Chemical erosion is when chemical substances such as acid rain erode the earth's features into smaller landforms.

Temperature erosion is when the temperature in an area is so extreme that it causes the earth to expand and crack into pieces, which can get carried away.

Erosion by people is when human actions such as land development and foot traffic can cause erosion.

Erosion shapes the landscape around us. A great example of erosion is the Grand Canyon. It was formed as the water of the Colorado River and wind carved away at the canyon walls over a period of 5 to 6 million years!

The Grand Canyon in the US was created by erosion.

 Complete the exercise.

Test your knowledge

Choose the best word to complete each sentence.

(1) The breaking up of earth and rocks into small pieces is called (weathering / erosion).

Ans.

(2) The carrying away of small pieces of rock, soil, and sand from one place to another is called (weathering / erosion).

Ans.

(3) Erosion caused by activities such as land development and foot traffic is erosion by (people / water).

Ans.

Chapter 2

Beach Erosion

What happens when erosion is sped up in a certain place, like a beach or coastline?

 Read the key points below. When you finish, check the box.

Key Points: Beach Erosion

Beach erosion is the loss of beach sand typically caused by water and wind movement. Sand is washed away from the beach, and moved farther out to sea or to another beach or coastline. This process can greatly reduce the size of a beach. Strong winds can also cause a beach to erode by blowing grains of sand away.

These factors are why hurricanes can be very bad for beaches. Hurricanes can produce strong winds and create big waves that wash away more sand from the beach than normal weathering does. It is very common to see severe erosion to beaches and coastlines after a hurricane or a strong thunderstorm.

Although beach erosion is mainly caused by natural weathering, there are times when human activities can lead to increased beach erosion. When people walk through the delicate grass or dune areas that often surround beaches, they can accidentally harm the native plants that grow there. As these native plants are damaged or removed, erosion can increase because the plant's roots help hold the beach sand in place. Without them, sand can be more easily carried away by wind or water.

Complete the exercise.

Test your knowledge

Answer T for true or F for false.

(1) Beach erosion is the increase of the size of a beach due to sand movement by wind and water.

Ans. ☐

(2) Strong winds may speed up erosion.

Ans. ☐

(3) Erosion can be stopped by removing plants native to a beach.

Ans. ☐

Chapter 2

Beach Erosion

Why do engineers study the effects of erosion?

Read the key points below. When you finish, check the box.

Key Points: Erosion Prevention

Erosion has been shaping coastlines for millions of years. The real problems come after a severe storm hits, when human activity speeds up erosion, or when buildings and roads are close enough to the ocean to be damaged by the effects of erosion. In some cases, beach erosion can cause flooding, and can even make a whole building collapse as the land it stands on is washed away.

Fortunately, scientists and engineers have studied erosion in order to create ways to help protect the environment, structures, and people from the damage it can cause. Here are some of the devices and methods that were developed to help communities that are facing problems due to erosion.

A house in danger of falling into the ocean because of beach erosion.

Redistributing Sand:
This method uses large trucks to bring in extra sand and dump it in the areas that are more prone to having sand washed away. This method is often used after hurricanes to help rebuild beaches.

Building windbreaks:
Windbreaks are fences that keep sand from blowing away in the wind. These fences can help keep a natural level of sand on the beach.

Using erosion control mats:
These mats stabilize the sand in an area long enough for plants to grow roots. The plant's roots help hold the sand and soil in place making it harder to erode away.

Complete the exercise.

Test your knowledge

Match the beach erosion prevention action with its definition.

A. Redistributing sand **B. Building windbreaks** **C. Using erosion control mats**

(1) They are designed to help grow native plants that hold beach sand in place.

Ans. ☐

(2) They prevent sand from being blown away by the wind.

Ans. ☐

(3) This method carries the sand by truck to a place where beach sand is likely to be washed away.

Ans. ☐

10

Chapter 2

Beach Erosion

Use the word box below to fill in the blanks and review key vocabulary.

Review the Key Points

The earth's features were shaped over many years by natural processes called weathering and erosion.

[ ] is the breaking down of rock and solid landforms into smaller pieces. [ ] is the process that transports the smaller pieces of rock, soil, and sand from one location to another. One of the main forces on Earth that causes erosion is water. Some other sources of erosion are wind, glacial, chemical, temperature, and human activities.

Beach erosion is the loss of [ ] typically caused by water and wind movement. Sand is washed away from the beach, and moved further out to sea or to another beach or coastline. This process can greatly reduce the size of a beach. [ ] can also cause a beach to erode by blowing grains of sand away.

Fortunately, scientists and engineers have studied erosion in order to create ways to help protect the environment, structures, and people from the damage it can cause.

beach sand / erosion / weathering / strong winds

Complete the exercise.

Math Mission

Answer the questions about erosion conditions to see how quickly erosion can change the landscape.

(1) Beaches on the south shore of New York's Long Island are eroding. About 2 feet of beach disappears each year. How many feet will erode in the next ten years?

Ans. [ ] feet

(2) If 6 inches of soil erode each year, how many years would it take for 36 inches of soil to erode from a hillside?

Ans. [ ] years

(3) Engineers are trying to rebuild a beach in North Carolina. If a dump truck can carry 4 tons of sand to add to the beach, how many truck loads would it take to bring 24 tons of sand to the beach?

Ans. [ ] trucks

Chapter 2

Beach Erosion

The Mission

You show up one summer to your favorite beach and find that a hurricane hit the beach during the year and eroded much of the beach away. Develop a plan to prevent the beach from eroding further and to help restore it to the way it was before.

Before you design...THINK!

1. Describe the mission in your own words.

2. Brainstorm a solution. Write your notes in the space below.
   Use the following questions to guide your thinking:

(1) What are some methods for preventing beach erosion that you read about in this chapter?
(2) What factors should you consider? Do you need to stop wind or water weathering?
Or can you design something to prevent the erosion in the first place?

12

Chapter 2

Beach Erosion

Read the mission. Then, draw and evaluate your solution.

The Mission

Develop a plan to prevent the beach from eroding further and to help restore it to the way it was before.

Design

Draw or write about your solution below.

Evaluate

Evaluate your design. What is one thing about your design that could be improved? Did you consider educating the community about how some erosion is caused by people as part of your plan?

13 Chapter 3

Tectonic Plates

Do you know why mountains rise so high above the earth's surface?

Read the key points. When you finish, check the box.

Key Points: What are Tectonic Plates?

Did you know the earth's outer layer, or crust, is not solid like an egg shell? Scientists have learned that the earth's crust is broken up into pieces called **tectonic plate**s that float on top of the **magma**, or hot melted rock, which makes up an inner layer of the earth called the **mantle**.

Continental Crust (8-40 km)
Upper Mantle (600 km)
Lower Mantle (2250 km)
Outer Core (2250 km)
Inner Core (1300 km)

Section of the earth's Crust

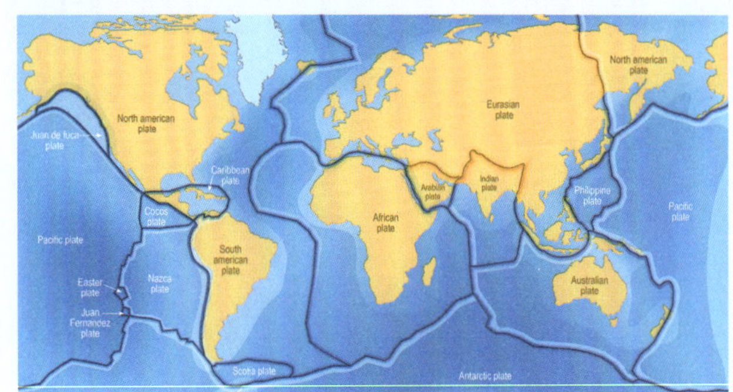

Tectonic Plates

When the earth's tectonic plates move, they create different features on the earth's surface. Their movement is responsible for most of the earth's features such as mountains and ocean trenches.

Tectonic plates can move against each other in different ways: they can slide past each other, slide over the top of each other, slide under each other, and move away from each other.

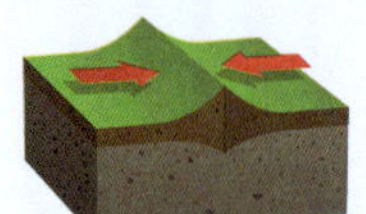

Plate Movement

Rocky Mountains in Colorado, USA

For example, two plates pushing up against each other has led to the creation of mountain ranges around the world, from the Rocky Mountains in North America to the Himalayan Mountains in Asia. When two plates move away from each other they can create trenches, like the deep Mariana Trench in the Pacific Ocean.

Complete the exercise.

Test your knowledge

Answer the questions using the passage for help.

(1) What are tectonic plates?

A. pieces of the earth's crust that fit together like a puzzle
B. the inner most layer of the earth
C. what mountains are made of
D. the layer of earth on the ocean floor

Ans. ☐

(2) Which is not a layer of the earth?

A. crust B. mantle C. sky D. core

Ans. ☐

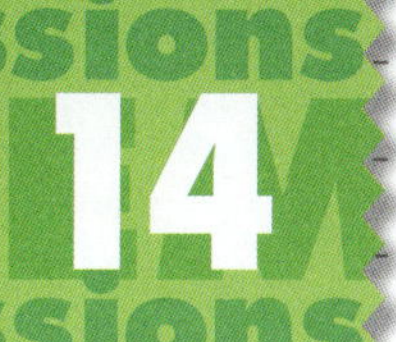

Chapter 3
Tectonic Plates

What causes an earthquake?

Read the key points below. When you finish, check the box.

Key Points: What is an earthquake?

Since the plates are floating on top of the moving magma that makes up the mantle, they are constantly moving and changing the earth's landscape and the ocean floors. This constant movement is what can lead to destructive events, like earthquakes.

An **earthquake** is an event caused when two plates slip past or rub against each other, under the earth's surface and create pressure. The point where they slip is called a **fault** or a **fault plane**. When enough pressure builds up along a fault plane an earthquake can occur. This causes the land around it to shake suddenly and violently which can cause major damage to everything surrounding it.

Cracked road after an earthquake

Earthquakes can destroy buildings, cause injuries, and cause changes to the land surrounding the fault zone.

There are some areas in the world that are more likely to experience earthquakes because these areas are along or near fault lines in the earth's crust. Some examples are the west coast of the United States, countries in the Pacific Ocean like Japan and Indonesia, and middle east countries like Turkey and Iran.

Buildings destroyed by an earthquake

Complete the exercise.

Test your knowledge

Answer the questions below based on the reading.

(1) What causes an earthquake?

A. the earth's rotation around the sun
B. the rise and fall of ocean tides
C. the pieces of the earth's crust moving against each other
D. the earth's gravity

Ans. [ ]

(2) What is a fault or fault plane?

A. a place where a mountain begins
B. a place where two plates move against each other
C. a place where the earth's crust separates
D. a place where there is no solid land

Ans. [ ]

(3) Why are some areas more likely to have an earthquake than others?

A. they have more solid land
B. they are along the ocean
C. they have more mountains
D. they are along fault lines in the earth's crust

Ans. [ ]

15

Chapter 3

Tectonic Plates

How can we help lessen earthquake damage?

Read the key points below. When you finish, check the box.

Key Points: Earthquake Safety

The most damage occurs at the center of the earthquake, or the **epicenter**. This is where an earthquake is the strongest. Since earthquakes cannot be predicted, scientists have developed tools to help measure their magnitude. Scientists use a device called a **seismograph** to measure the movement and vibrations, or seismic waves of earthquakes. The length of the lines recorded shows the size of the seismic waves and the strength of the earthquake that caused them. It is important to study the strength and vibrations of an earthquake, so we can determine how to help keep communities safe when they occur.

In communities where earthquakes are more likely to happen, like southern California, scientists and engineers work together to make buildings stronger and help lessen the damage caused by an earthquake. Here are a few examples:

One traditional way to help prevent earthquake damage to a building is by reinforcing the structure. This is typically done with shear walls, cross-beams, and horizontal frames that help keep the building stable during seismic waves.

Another option is to build a flexible foundation using rubber, lead, and steel underneath a building that will absorb the seismic waves and help the building stay stable.

Seismic rings are a newer option for earthquake protection. They are made of plastic or concrete and are placed underground around a building. They are designed to help channel the shock waves from an earthquake and move them around the building instead of through it.

Reinforced Building with Steel Braces

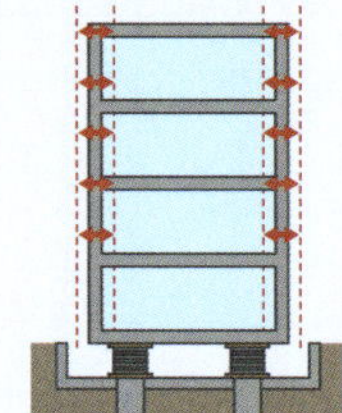

Rubber Material Seismic Isolation Device Under a Building

Complete the exercise.

Test your knowledge

Answer the questions below about the reading.

(1) Where does most earthquake damage occur?

A. the fault plane B. the epicenter C. the furthest from the epicenter

Ans. ☐

(2) What is a seismograph?

A. a device used to measure seismic waves
B. a device used to measure earthquake damage
C. a device used to predict earthquakes
D. a device used to measure the distance an earthquake travels

Ans. ☐

16

Chapter 3
Tectonic Plates

Use the word box below to fill in the blanks and review key vocabulary.

Review the Key Points

Scientists have learned that the earth's crust is broken up into pieces called tectonic plates that float on top of the magma, or hot melted rock, which makes up an inner layer of the earth called the [ ].

When the earth's tectonic plates move, they create different features on the earth's surface. Their movement is responsible for most of the earth's features such as mountains and ocean trenches.

[ ] can move against each other in different ways: they can slide past each other, slide over the top of each other, slide under each other, and move away from each other.

An [ ] is an event caused when two plates slip past or rub against each other, under the earth's surface and create pressure. The point where they slip is called a fault or a fault plane. When enough pressure builds up along a fault plane an earthquake can occur. This causes the land around it to shake suddenly and violently which can cause major damage to everything surrounding it.

The most damage occurs at the center of the earthquake, or the [ ]. This is where an earthquake is the strongest. Since earthquakes cannot be predicted, scientists have developed tools to help measure their magnitude. Scientists use a device called a [ ] to measure the movement and vibrations, or seismic waves of earthquakes. The length of the lines recorded shows the size of the seismic waves and the strength of the earthquake that caused them. It is important to study the strength and vibrations of an earthquake, so we can determine how to help keep communities safe when they occur.

epicenter / earthquake / mantle / tectonic plates / seismograph

Complete the exercise.

Math Mission

Scientists are constantly reviewing graphs and charts of old earthquake activity to help them better understand earthquakes and how to keep people safe. Use the chart to answer the questions below.

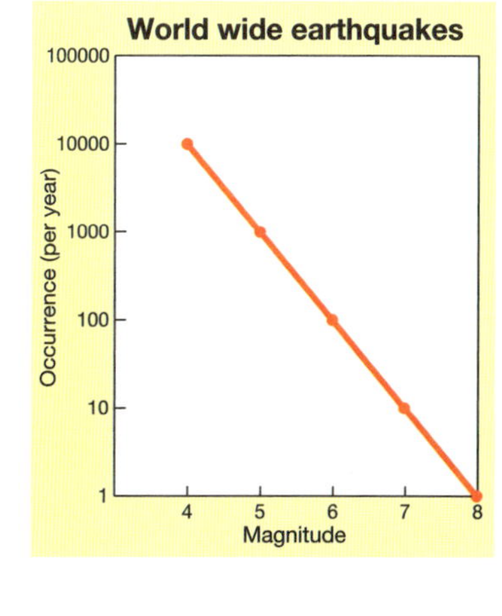

(1) How many magnitude 5 earthquakes happen each year?

Ans. [ ]

(2) What magnitude earthquakes happen the most often?

A. magnitude 4 B. magnitude 6 C. magnitude 8

Ans. [ ]

(3) What magnitude earthquakes happen the least often?

A. magnitude 4 B. magnitude 6 C. magnitude 8

Ans. [ ]

Chapter 3

Tectonic Plates

Read the mission. Then, answer the following questions to help you with your solution.

The Mission

Imagine you live in a community that is at high risk for earthquake activity. Design a way to prevent damage to your home from an earthquake.
You can make changes to your home, the land around it, or the tools you will use.

Before you design...THINK!

1. Describe the mission in your own words.

2. Brainstorm about a solution. Write your notes in the space below.
   Use the following questions to guide your thinking:

(1) What type of prevention technology would you use?
(2) Can you improve on current devices? Or create a new solution?

18

Chapter 3

Tectonic Plates

Read the mission. Then, draw and evaluate your solution.

The Mission

Design a way to prevent damage to your home from an earthquake. You can make changes to your home, the land around it, or the tools you will use.

Design

Draw or write your solution below.

Evaluate

Consider your solution: What technology did you use to help reinforce your dwelling? Did you improve on something that already exists? Or did you invent your own solution?

19

Chapter 4

Flooding

What is a flood? And what causes a flood?

Read the key points. When you finish, check the box.

Key Points: What causes flooding?

Do you remember playing in puddles after a rainstorm when you were younger? Puddles often form when there is too much rain for the ground to absorb or there is nowhere for the water to drain. While small puddles are fun to play in, too much rain can be dangerous. When rain falls and it isn't absorbed by the ground or has no place to drain, it can cause a **flood**. A flood is a type of natural disaster that happens when water quickly covers land that is usually dry.

Flooding is caused by heavy rain from severe storms as you learned in Chapter 1. But, it can also be caused by a large amount of snow melting quickly, overflowing rivers, and other severe weather events such as hurricanes.

There are different types of floods. Some can be good for an area while others can be devastating.

A river flood happens when the banks or sides of a river overflow. This can damage nearby streets, cars, and buildings. However, rivers in some areas do flood each year and help create land that is good for farming. Flood waters can carry nutrients that enrich the soil.

A flash flood happens when heavy rainfall causes a lot of water to flow through a river or stream very fast. Flash floods can also happen in city streets, if rain falls too fast for drainage systems to keep up. This type of flood is very dangerous because it can happen so quickly that people do not have time to get to safety and can get swept away and injured by the fast moving water.

A coastal flood happens when storms cause the water along a coastline to rise above the beach level. This can cause damage to beaches and manmade structures.

Complete the exercise.

Test your knowledge

Choose one of the following sentences that contains errors.

A. Floods can occur when a lot of rain falls and the rain is not absorbed by the ground.

B. Floods are not caused by severe weather events like hurricanes.

C. There are various types of floods, such as river floods, flash floods, and coastal floods.

Ans.

Chapter 4
Flooding

What are some problems flooding can cause?

Read the key points below. When you finish, check the box.

Key Points: Effects of Floods

Flooding can be disastrous for communities. Below are some examples of the problems flooding can cause.

Effects of Floods on Structures:
Flood waters can cause mold to grow in houses and buildings. This can cause houses to rot, which can make structures unsafe for people to live in or work in.

Effects of Floods on Water Supplies:
Flooding can also damage sewer systems and cause waste to get into a community's drinking water supplies. This can make people sick if they drink contaminated water.

Effects of Floods on Human Health:
Floods can bring pests, like mosquitoes who like to lay their eggs in still water. These pests can multiply quickly and carry diseases like the Zika virus or malaria which can make people very sick.

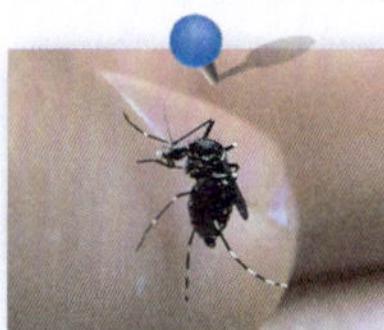

Mosquitoes can carry diseases

Effects of Floods on the Environment:
Flood waters can sometimes be helpful to the areas around them. When a river floods, it leaves behind nutrients that soak into the soil and create good farmland. A floodplain is an area surrounding a river that naturally absorbs flood waters.

Mississippi River floodplain

Complete the exercise.

Test your knowledge

Match each problem caused by flooding to the dangerous effects it can have on people.

(1) mosquitoes 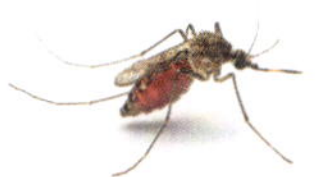 ●

(2) mold and rot  ●

(3) damaged sewer systems  ●

● contaminated drinking water

● diseases like the Zika virus or malaria

● structures that are unsafe to live in

21

Chapter 4

Flooding

What are some ways we can protect ourselves from flooding?

Read the key points below. When you finish, check the box.

Key Points: Ways to Prevent Flood Damage

Engineers have designed systems to control flooding such as dams, levees, and dikes that help keep fast-moving and dangerous flood waters away from buildings and structures. By stopping flood waters or controlling their movement, we can keep our communities safe.

Dams:
A dam is a wall or structure designed to hold back water or prevent it from flowing. One side of a dam often forms a reservoir, a type of lake that stores water for people to use. Reservoirs supply communities with water and power.

Levees:
A levee is an embankment or ridge built to stop a river from overflowing its banks onto dry land. Some levees are created naturally by soil and rocks that are deposited on a river's banks as it flows. A levee can also be manmade, by building up the sides of a river with dirt, sand, or cement.

Dikes:
A dike is a long wall or ditch built to prevent flood waters from damaging surrounding communities. Dikes are built to protect communities where flood water might naturally accumulate or drain into land now inhabited by people.

Complete the exercise.

Test your knowledge

Match the type of flood barrier to its definition.

(1) A wall or structure built across a body of water to hold water back.

(2) A long wall or ditch built to prevent flood water from flooding an area.

(3) An embankment, natural or manmade, built to stop a river from overflowing its banks.

- dam 
- levee 
- dike 

22 Chapter 4

Flooding

Use the word box below to fill in the blanks and review key vocabulary.

Review the Key Points

When rain falls and it isn't absorbed by the ground or has no place to drain, it can cause a ________. A flood is a type of natural disaster that happens when water quickly covers land that is usually dry.

Flooding is caused by ________ from severe storms as you learned in Chapter 1. But, it can also be caused by a large amount of snow melting quickly, overflowing rivers, and other severe weather events such as hurricanes.

Flooding can be disastrous for communities and cause harm to structures, water supplies, and people's health.

Flood waters can sometimes be helpful to the areas around them. When a river floods, it leaves behind nutrients that soak into the soil and create good farmland. A ________ is an area surrounding a river that naturally absorbs flood waters.

Engineers have designed systems to control flooding such as dams (a wall or structure designed to hold water or prevent it from flowing), levees (an embankment or ridge built to stop a river from overflowing), and ________ (a long wall or ditch built to stop flood waters) that help keep fast moving and dangerous flood waters away from buildings and structures. By stopping flood waters or controlling their movement we can keep our communities safe.

heavy rain / floodplain / dikes / flood

Complete the exercise.

Math Mission

The map to the right shows which areas have a higher risk of flooding due to how close they are to shore. Answer the question below using the map. Remember on a map distance is always to scale: 1 cm = 100 m.

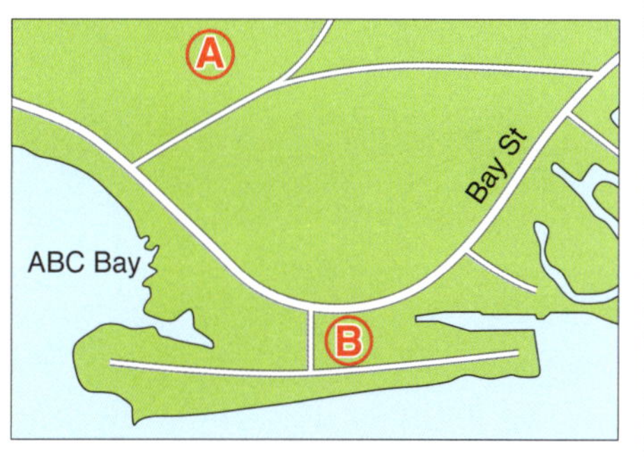

(1) Which of the locations, A and B, on the map is less likely to be at risk of flooding?

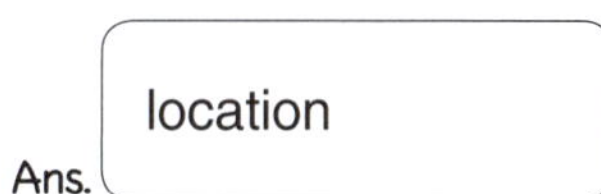

Ans. location ________

(2) If the distance between locations A and B is 3 centimeters (cm) on the map, how many meters (m) is the actual distance?

Ans. ________ m

(3) When the actual distance between location A on the map and location C, which is not shown on the map, is 500 meters away, how many centimeters is distance on the map?

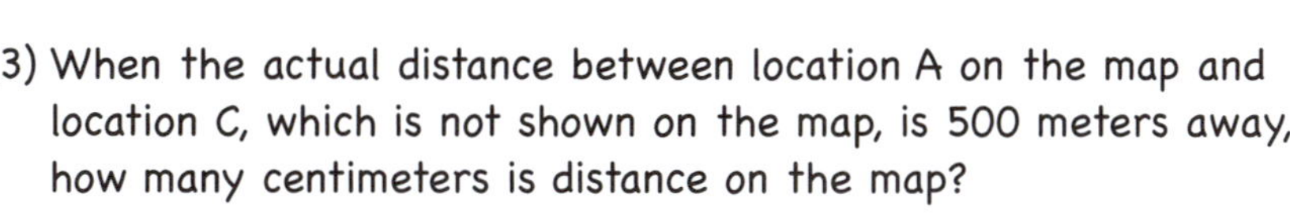
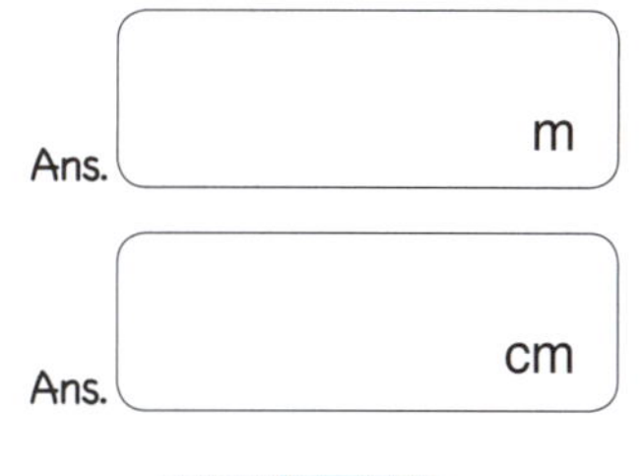

Ans. ________ cm

23 Chapter 4 Flooding

Read the mission. Then, answer the following questions to help you with your solution.

The Mission

Imagine you live near a large river that commonly floods. Design a new piece of technology or develop a plan to prevent some of the possible problems caused by flooding that you learned about it this chapter.

Before you design...THINK!

1. Describe the mission in your own words.

2. Brainstorm about a solution. Write your notes in the space below. Use the following questions to guide your thinking:

(1) Can you use existing flood prevention tools in your plan? Or will you need to develop a new tool?

(2) What type of flooding problem do you want to focus on?

Chapter 4

Flooding

Read the mission. Then, draw and evaluate your solution.

The Mission

Imagine you live near a large river that commonly floods. Design a new piece of technology or develop a plan to prevent some of the possible problems caused by flooding that you learned about it this chapter.

Design

Draw or about write your solution below.

Evaluate

Evaluate your flood prevention or protection system. Do you think it would work? Why or why not? Can you think of anything else you could add to make your plan more successful?

25

Chapter 5

Changing Climates

What is climate? What causes different areas to have different climates?

Read the key points. When you finish, check the box.

Key Points: What is climate?

Climate is the pattern of weather over a period of time in a certain area. For example, the climate near the equator is warm and wet for most of the year. Climate does not change from day to day like weather, as you learned in Chapter 1. An area's climate is specific to its location and the people, animals, and plants that live there are adapted to their climates.

There are several things that affect the climate of an area. These factors are the landscape of an area, how close or far from bodies of water like lakes or oceans an area is, an area's latitude, or location on the earth's surface, and an area's height above sea level. These factors cause changes to the temperature, humidity, wind speed, or the type and amount of precipitation, such as rain or snow, that an area gets.

The distance above sea level is an important factor in determining an area's climate. The higher the area is above sea level, the colder and drier it often is, like Denver, CO in the U.S. Places that are closer to sea level typically have more warm and wet weather like the Hawaiian Islands in the U.S.

Denver, CO USA

Hawaiian Islands, USA

Complete the exercise.

Test your knowledge

Answer T for true or F for false.

(1) The climate is the weather pattern in a specific area, and it changes daily like the weather. Ans.

(2) The latitude of an area on the earth is one of the factors that affects the local climate. Ans.

(3) The higher the area is above sea level, the more warm and dry it tends to be. Ans.

26

Chapter 5

Changing Climates

What type of climate do you live in? Do you have hot summers or freezing winters? A lot rain or very little rain?

Read the key points below. When you finish, check the box.

Key Points: Climates around the World

There are different types of climates around the world such as Polar, Temperate, Tropical, Continental, Dry, and others.

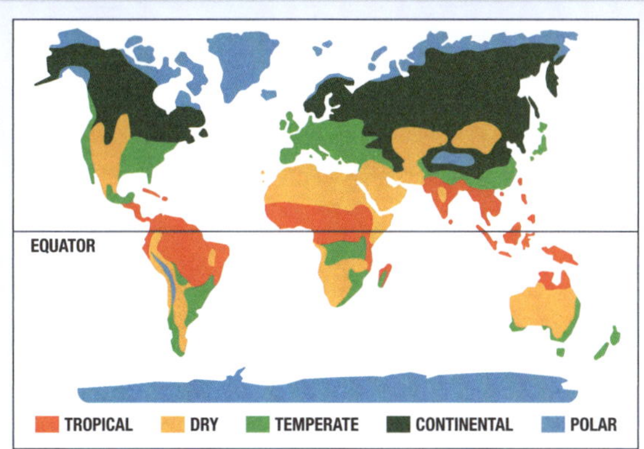

Polar Climate Zone
- cold temperatures all year
- short summers and long winters
- warm months are less than 50 °F degrees
- Examples: Northern coastal regions of North America, Greenland, and Antarctica

Temperate Climate Zone
- hot summers and cold winters
- four distinct seasons
- varying precipitation rain, snow, sleet...etc.
- Examples: New England in North America and Central Europe

Tropical Climate Zone
- large amounts of rainfall each year
- warm and wet for most of the year
- closest to the equator
- Average temp: greater than 64 °F year round
- Examples: South America, Hawaiian Island in NA, and parts of Africa

Dry Climate Zone
- dry and arid conditions
- less than 12 inches of rain per year
- Examples: Southern North America, Africa, and Australia

Continental Climate Zone
- Warm to cool summers and very cold winters
- Intense snowstorms, strong winds and temperatures below −22 °F
- Examples: the Polar Climate in places like Canada in the North America and Russia in Europe

Other Climate Zones – These main climate zones can be separated into smaller categories like:
- **Highland Zone** - where temperature and weather changes quickly as the distance above sea level rises
- **Subtropics Zone** - where the temperature is more mild than humid tropics, with less rainfall
- **Coastal Zone** - where there are cool winters and warm summers and the temperature does not get too hot or too cold

Complete the exercise.

Test your knowledge

Match the climate zone to the example pictured below.

A. polar climate B. temperate climate C. tropical climate D. dry climate

(1)

Ans.

(2)

Ans.

(3)

Ans.

(4)

Ans.

27

Chapter 5

Changing Climates

Since climate is the weather of an area over time, can it change like the weather does?

Read the key points below. When you finish, check the box.

Key Points: What causes climates to change?

According to the National Oceanic and Atmospheric Association, or NOAA, climates all over the world are changing. Polar climates that were once never warmer than 50 °F in the summer are now seeing summer temperatures of 65 °F and higher. This is due to a process called global warming.

Global warming is a process that causes the average temperature on Earth to increase or warm up because of extra gas trapped in the atmosphere. When too many of these gases like carbon dioxide, methane, ozone, nitrous oxide and others are in the atmosphere, they trap the sun's heat and the temperature of the earth begins to rise. This is called the **greenhouse effect**. This change in our global climate has a negative effect on people, animals, and plants around world because we are all adapted to, or prepared for, the climates we live in. Scientists believe this process is also causing more severe weather events like thunderstorms, hurricanes, droughts, and forest fires. This can make our living conditions on Earth unstable.

While no one is 100% sure what is causing the earth's atmosphere to warm up, most scientists believe it's because of the pollution created by people's actions.

When we burn fossil fuels like coal and oil to create energy, as you'll learn in Chapter 7, we are adding to the greenhouse gases. So when we use gas to drive a car or burn coal to cook dinner we are adding to the pollution that causes global warming.

Another factor that could be adding to the rising global temperatures is deforestation, or the clearing of trees and plants from large areas so people can build on it. Trees and plants are what turn the carbon dioxide we breathe out back into oxygen we can breathe in. With less trees and plants less carbon dioxide is changed and it instead adds to the air pollution that is warming the atmosphere.

Complete the exercise.

Test your knowledge

Answer T for true or F for false.

(1) Global warming is a process that causes the average temperature on Earth to increase or warm up because of extra gas trapped in the atmosphere.

Ans.

(2) The various actions of people have no effect on global warming at all.

Ans.

(3) The extra gases in the atmosphere have a negative impact on the earth by trapping the sun's heat and causing the earth's temperature to start rising.

Ans.

28 Chapter 5

Changing Climates

Use the word box below to fill in the blanks and review key vocabulary.

Review the Key Points

[   ] is the pattern of weather over a period of time in a certain area. Climate does not change from day to day like weather, as you learned in Chapter 1. An area's climate is specific to its location and the people, animals, and plants that live there are adapted to their climates.

There are several things that affect the climate of an area. These factors are the landscape of an area, how close or far from bodies of water like lakes or oceans an area is, an area's latitude, or location on the earth's surface, and an area's height above [   ]. These factors cause changes to the temperature, humidity, wind speed, or the type and amount of precipitation, such as rain or snow, that an area gets.

There are different types of climates around the world such as Polar, Temperate, Tropical, Continental, Dry, and others.

[   ] is a process that causes the average temperature on Earth to increase or warm up because of extra gas trapped in the atmosphere. When too many of these gases like carbon dioxide, methane, ozone, nitrous oxide and others are in the atmosphere, they trap the sun's heat and the temperature of the earth begins to rise. This is called the [   ]. This change in our global climate has a negative effect on people, animals, and plants around world because we are all adapted to, or prepared for, the climates we live in.

While no one is 100% sure what is causing the earth's atmosphere to warm up, most scientists believe it's because of the pollution created by people's actions.

greenhouse effect / sea level / global warming / climate

Complete the exercise.

Math Mission

A plan is being implemented to restore the forest by planting seedlings in areas where many trees are cut down each year. It takes three minutes for one adult to plant a single sapling. Answer the following questions.

(1) How long does it take an adult to plant five saplings?

Ans. [   ] minutes

(2) How many saplings can an adult plant in 60 minutes?

Ans. [   ] saplings

(3) How many saplings can three adults plant in 30 minutes?

Ans. [   ] saplings

29 Chapter 5
Changing Climates

Read the mission. Then, answer the following questions to help you with your solution.

The Mission

Climate change has a negative effect on our environment. Rising temperatures can hurt us, the earth, and plants and animals around us. Create a plan to help inform the people in your community about climate zones and climate change.

Before you design...THINK!

1. Describe the mission in your own words.

2. Brainstorm about a solution. Write your notes in the space below.
   Use the following questions to guide your thinking:

(1) How can you inform your town about the dangers of global warming?
(2) How would you get everyone to follow your plan?

Chapter 5

Changing Climates

Read the mission. Then, draw and evaluate your solution.

The Mission

Climate change has a negative effect on our environment. Rising temperatures can hurt us, the earth, and plants and animals around us. Create a plan to help inform the people in your community about climate zones and climate change.

Design

Draw or write your solution below.

Evaluate

How would your plan work? Do you think you would be successful? What is something you can change about your plan?

31 Chapter 6
Landslides

Do you know what a landslide is?

Read the key points. When you finish, check the box.

Key Points: What is a landslide?

Have you ever built a tower out of blocks, and as you went to stack the last block on top, you bumped the tower, causing all the blocks to come crashing down? This experience is similar to what happens when a landslide occurs.

A **landslide** is a large movement of material, such as rock, soil, or mud, down the slope of a hill, a cliff, or a mountainside. And, just like your falling block tower, landslides can happen suddenly, due to changes in the stability or strength of their slopes. Although, sometimes land moves slowly down a mountainside over a longer period of time.

When a landslide happens it can cause serious damage to the surrounding land and communities, by blocking roads and burying buildings. Landslides are one of the most dangerous natural events because they can happen anywhere in the world. They can occur on every type of surface, from hard rock to soft sand, and can even happen on underwater slopes.

A landslide can travel down a slope at speeds up to 35 miles per hour! That's about as fast as you can ride your bike downhill! Anything that gets in the way of a landslide, from trees to cars, will get carried along as it goes.

Complete the exercise.

Test your knowledge

Answer T for true or F for false.

(1) Landslides are often caused by natural factors, such as heavy rain or earthquakes.

Ans. 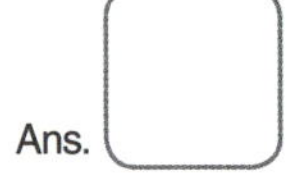

(2) Landslides do not occur suddenly because hard rocks and soil always move slowly down a slope.

Ans. 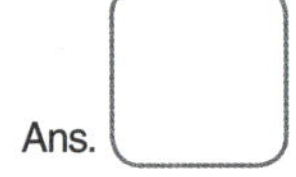

(3) Landslides can cause rocks and soil to slide across roads and buildings, causing serious damage.

Ans. 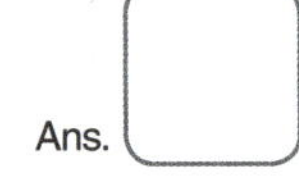

32 Chapter 6 Landslides

Can human activity increase the chances of a landslide happening?

Read the key points below. When you finish, check the box.

Key Points: Landslide Causes

There are multiple factors that can affect the stability of a slope, but gravity plays a big part in causing loose rocks and soil to slide. **Gravity**, or the force that pulls all objects toward the earth, is a common factor in natural events like landslides. It is the same force that brought down the block tower.

Gravity isn't the only force that brought down the block tower. Just like when you bumped the tower, and added another force to the situation, landslides also need a second force, or trigger, other than gravity to happen. The actions below can all create an unstable slope that is more vulnerable to landslides.

Natural Hazards:
Other natural hazards such as earthquakes or volcanic eruptions, like you learned about in Chapter 3, can also create higher chances of landslides.

When an **earthquake** hits an area it can shake loose soil and rock from the sides of mountains or hills and cause a strong landslide.

When a volcano erupts, it causes dirt, mud, and ash to slide down its sides, and this can destroy nearby houses, roads and communities.

Rainfall:
Heavy rain is a major cause of landslides. It can cause soil and rocks to loosen and slide down a slope. Rainfall can also cause erosion which can be a contributing factor to a landslide. If rain erodes the mountainside or hillside, a slope can become steeper which can lead to a higher chance of landslides.

Rock Type:
Sometimes the type of rock in an area can increase the chances of a landslide. If the rock is soft like limestone, it could be eroded or loosened more easily than a harder type of rock. This leads to more unstable slopes where landslides can happen.

Construction:
Human activity such as construction or demolition can damage nearby land and lead to landslides. Human activity like deforestation can also leave hillsides vulnerable to landslides because there are fewer plant roots to help hold soil and rocks in place .

Complete the exercise.

Test your knowledge

Choose three actions that can raise the risk of landslides.

A. heavy rain

B. high temperatures

C. earthquakes

D. demolition and construction

Ans. ___ , ___ , ___

33 Chapter 6

Landslides

What should you do if a landslide occurs in your area?

Read the key points below. When you finish, check the box.

Key Points: Landslide Prevention and Safety

Since landslides can happen suddenly, it is important to be aware of areas where landslides might occur. Scientists and engineers often monitor such areas. They measure the rainfall in an area and how steep the slopes are to help determine if a landslide is likely to occur.

They also look for physical signs that show an area's risk of having a landslide, such as ground that is cracking or buckling where it hasn't before, places where telephone poles or deck beams are tilting, or areas where the road or land appears to be sinking.

To help prevent landslides, engineers have developed technologies such as nets, anchors, and retaining walls to support slopes that are at risk.

Nets – help prevent rocks and debris from falling onto roads.

Anchors – are drilled into at risk slopes to help hold and stabilize the land.

Retaining Walls – are built to keep unstable slopes from falling onto roadways or structures.

In case prevention efforts don't work, it is also important for people to develop evacuation plans should a landslide happen in their area. When you develop an evacuation plan, you need a safe place to go and also to make sure you have essential supplies you can carry with you. Remember, people need food, water, and shelter to survive. It is also a good idea to have first aid equipment in case someone is hurt.

Complete the exercise.

Test your knowledge

Which of the following contains an error?

A. Engineers have developed nets, anchors and walls to prevent landslides.

B. Since landslides occur suddenly, it is useless for people to make evacuation plans.

C. When planning an evacuation plan in an emergency, we should make sure that we have the supplies needed to survive, such as water and food. In addition, it is necessary to know in advance of a safe place to go to.

Ans. ☐

Chapter 6

Landslides

Use the word box below to fill in the blanks and review key vocabulary.

Review the Key Points

A [ ] is a large movement of material, such as rock, soil, or mud, down the slope of a hill, a cliff, or a mountainside. Landslides can happen suddenly, due to changes in the stability or strength of their [ ]. Although, sometimes land moves slowly down a mountainside over a longer period of time.

When a landslide happens it can cause serious damage to the surrounding land and communities, by blocking roads and burying buildings. Landslides are one of the most dangerous natural events because they can happen anywhere in the world.

There are multiple factors that can affect the stability of a slope, but [ ] plays a big part in causing loose rocks and soil to slide. Gravity, or the force that pulls all objects toward the earth, is a common factor in natural events like landslides.

Landslides also need a second force, or trigger, other than gravity to happen. (e.g. natural hazards, rainfall, type of rock, and construction)

Since landslides can happen suddenly, it is important to be aware of areas where landslides might occur. Scientists and engineers often [ ] such areas.

Engineers have developed technologies such as nets, anchors, and retaining walls to support slopes that are at risk.

In case prevention efforts don't work, it is also important for people to develop [ ] plans should a landslide happen in their area.

slopes / monitor / gravity / landslide / evacuation

Complete the exercise.

Math Mission

City Z has received heavy rains in the two days since May 5, and residents are worried about the possibility of landslides. The graphs on the right show precipitation on May 5 and 6 on slopes A, B and C.

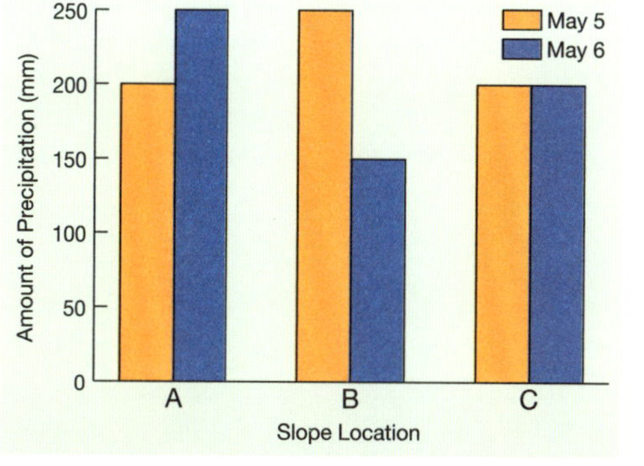

(1) What was the precipitation on Slope A on May 5?

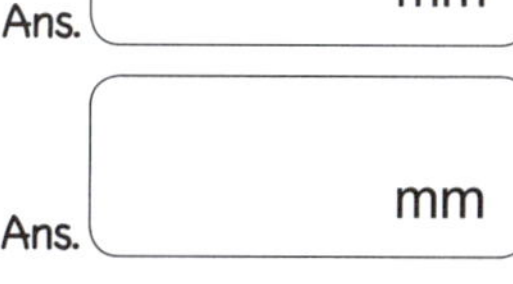

Ans. [ ] mm

(2) What was the precipitation on Slope B on May 6?

Ans. [ ] mm

(3) What was the amount of precipitation in two days on Slope C?

Ans. [ ] mm

(4) Which slope had the highest amount of precipitation in two days?

Ans. [ ]

35

Chapter 6

Landslides

Read the mission. Then, answer the following questions to help you with your solution.

The Mission

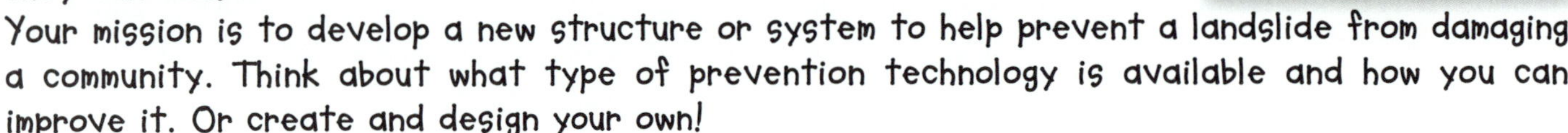

Landslides can be harmful to people and communities. Engineers have developed different ways to prevent them and help lessen the damage they can cause.
Your mission is to develop a new structure or system to help prevent a landslide from damaging a community. Think about what type of prevention technology is available and how you can improve it. Or create and design your own!

Before you design...THINK!

1. Describe the mission in your own words.

2. Brainstorm your solution. Write your notes in the space below.
   Use the following questions to guide your thinking:

(1) Would you use existing technology in your design? Or do you want to create something new to improve protection?
(2) What type of materials could you use? Would it be better to use rigid materials or flexible materials?

Chapter 6

Landslides

Read the mission. Then, draw and evaluate your solution.

The Mission

Your mission is to develop a tool or system to help prevent a landslide from damaging your town. Think about what type of prevention technology is available or create and design your own!

Design

Draw or write your solution below.

Evaluate

Evaluate your landslide protection or prevention system. Do you think it would work? Why or why not? Do you think you need to include safety precautions or evacuation plans along with your device?

37

Chapter 7

Natural Resources for Energy

What do you think when you hear the phrase "natural resources"?

Read the key points. When you finish, check the box.

Key Points: Natural Resources

Ever wonder where the gasoline to power a car comes from? Or how water can be used to power a generator?

A lot of the energy we use every day comes from natural resources. Natural resources are different resources that exist in nature. We use them to power our cars, homes, toys, and most other devices around us.

Some examples of natural resources we use are: coal, oil, wood, water, sunlight, and wind. Here you will learn more about coal and oil, two of the natural resources we use most often to power our world.

Coal: Coal is different from rocks made of only minerals. Coal is made of plant matter, and undergoes many changes before it becomes the black and shiny substance we burn for fuel. While it looks like a normal rock, it is actually made of plants which grew hundreds of millions of years ago, and were put under extreme pressure at the bottom of lakes and swamps. The pressure they were under was so intense it changed the physical material in the plants and minerals into coal. Nowadays, we dig the coal up from where it was created and use it as a fuel source.

Oil: Oil is made of the remains of ancient living things that slowly piled up on the bottom of the ocean and were covered by sediment and sand. This made it possible for bacteria in the soil along with extreme heat and pressure to change the material into oil. Oil is found underground . It is extracted with giant drilling machines that are strong enough penetrate into the earth. When oil comes out of the ground, it usually looks black or dark brown.

Complete the exercise.

Test your knowledge

(1) Which would be considered a natural resource commonly used for energy?

A. wood B. glass C. fabric D. plastic

Ans.

(2) Which of the following is a natural resources that comes from plants that died millions of years ago?

A. wood B. plastic C. coal D. wind

Ans.

Chapter 7

Natural Resources for Energy

What are the advantages and disadvantages of natural non-renewable resources such as coal and oil?

 Read the key points below. When you finish, check the box. 

Key Points: Issues with Non-renewable Resources

The way we get these natural resources and turn them into energy is different for each resource. Coal and oil can supply us with a lot of energy, but getting them can also cause problems.

Digging for coal can be unsafe for miners. Miners breathe in coal dust as they work which can cause illnesses later in life. They can also get trapped in a mine if it collapses. Additionally, in order to use coal as a source of energy, it has to be burned. This adds to air pollution, which can have negative impacts on the earth's atmosphere as you read in Chapter 5.

There are problems involved in drilling for oil too. Drilling can sometimes cause oil spills, which are harmful to the environment, especially to the plants and animals that live nearby. And like coal, oil needs to be burned to release energy and that causes harmful air pollution.

Another major problem with some natural resources such as coal and oil is that they are non-renewable. A **non-renewable resource** is a natural resource that is gone forever once it is used up. When coal or oil are burned they are converted into other substances which release energy and cannot be turned back into their original form and used again.

Complete the exercise.

Test your knowledge

Answer T for true or F for false.

(1) Coal and oil have the advantage of providing us with a lot of energy.

Ans. ☐

(2) Coal and oil have the disadvantage of causing air pollution because they have to be burned to produce energy.

Ans. ☐

(3) Coal and oil have the advantage of being reusable natural resources.

Ans. ☐

39

Chapter 7

Natural Resources for Energy

Do you know which natural resources are renewable?

Read the key points below. When you finish, check the box.

Key Points: Renewable Resources

Since there are problems with non-renewable natural resources like coal and oil, scientists and engineers have developed ways to use renewable resources for energy instead. **Renewable resources** are resources that can be used repeatedly and are replaced naturally.

Some examples of renewable resources are wind, solar or sun, and water.

Water or Hydropower:
Hydropower is power produced by using the energy created by running water. For example, water flowing in a river can be used to spin a wheel in a machine called a generator. The generator converts the energy of the moving water to electricity. People will often build dams to block and control the flow of water in a river and use it to power generators. But, hydropower can be created anywhere there is running water.

Wind Power:
Wind power is created by harnessing wind. When wind turns the blades of a windmill, a generator converts the energy of the spinning blades into power we can use. Wind is a renewable natural resource because we can never run out of wind!

Solar Power:
Solar power is created using sunlight. Solar panels are used to capture energy from the sun's rays and turn it into power for your home.

Complete the exercise.

Test your knowledge

Match effective ways to convert each renewable resource to usable energy.

(1) water or hydropower ●　　　　● solar panel 

(2) wind power ●　　　　● dam 

(3) solar power ●　　　　● windmill 

40

Chapter 7

Natural Resources for Energy

Use the word box below to fill in the blanks and review key vocabulary.

Review the Key Points

A lot of the energy we use every day comes from [   ] resources. Natural resources are different resources that exist in nature. We use them to power our cars, homes, toys, and most other devices around us.

Some examples of natural resources we use are: coal, oil, wood, water, sunlight, and wind.

The way we get these natural resources and turn them into [   ] is different for each resource. Coal and [   ] can supply us with a lot of energy, but getting them can also cause problems.

When coal or oil are burned they are converted into other substances which release energy and cannot be turned back into their [   ] form and used again.

Since there are problems with non-renewable natural resources like coal and oil, scientists and engineers have developed ways to use [   ] resources for energy instead. Renewable resources are resources that can be used repeatedly and are replaced naturally.

original / natural / renewable / energy / oil

Complete the exercise.

Math Mission

Answer the following questions about Renewable energy.

(1) There are residential solar panels with a power generation capacity of 100 kW per panel. How many kilowatts of power will be generated when you install eight of these? "kW (kilowatt)" is a unit of electric power.

Ans. [   ] kW

(2) One windmill can produce enough electricity to power 1,500 homes for a year. How many windmills does it take to produce enough electricity to power 4,500 homes for a year?

Ans. [   ] windmills

Chapter 7

Natural Resources for Energy

Read the mission. Then, answer the following questions to help you with your solution.

The Mission

Think about where you live. What natural resources near you could be used for energy? Do you think your area could benefit from using renewable natural resources?
Design a plan to bring renewable energy to or to increase the use of renewable energy in your area.

Before you design...THINK!

1. Describe the mission in your own words.

2. Brainstorm about a solution. Write your notes in the space below.
Use the following questions to guide your thinking:

(1) What natural resources are plentiful in your area?
(2) Does your town already use renewable energy resources? How can you improve on the use of renewable resources?
(3) If your area does not use renewable energy sources, how can you get people to use them?

42 Chapter 7 Natural Resources for Energy

Read the mission. Then, draw and evaluate your solution.

The Mission

Design a plan to bring renewable energy to or to increase the use of renewable energy in your area.

Design

Draw or write about your solution below.

Evaluate

Evaluate your plan. How can you get more people to participate in your plan? Do you think people will want to help you with your plan? What do you want the outcome of your plan to be?

43

Chapter 8

Disposing of Waste

What do you do with things you no longer need?

 Read the key points. When you finish, check the box.

Key Points: What is waste?

Do you ever think about what happens to the scrap paper you used for your math homework and then threw away? It will probably be thrown out with the rest of your garbage. Objects like used paper, discarded food and other things you throw away are called **waste**.

We can find a variety of waste in our everyday lives. When you eat a banana you typically throw the peel away when you're done. You do the same thing with the wrapper from a candy bar. Both get thrown in the trash when you have finished your snack, but there is one big difference between these two pieces of waste.

The banana peel will decay, or break down, over a few months and its nutrients can be used by the soil. The candy bar wrapper will not break down as quickly. It is made of plastic which can take 20 years or more to break down and will not add any nutrients to the soil.

Most of the waste or trash humans throw out is not **biodegradable** like the banana peel, and will not naturally break down into the soil. Paper, plastic, and glass all take a long time to break down when they are thrown away. They are non-biodegradable, because even when they break down they are not adding nutrients to the earth. When biodegradable and non-biodegradable materials are thrown out together it can slow down the natural break-down of the biodegradable material.

In the US alone, people make around 1 million pounds of waste materials each year! Can you imagine how much waste that is?

 Complete the exercise.

Test your knowledge

Choose all of the following waste materials that are not biodegradable (do not decay or break down naturally) and will accumulate without being able to nourish the soil.

A. plastic B. banana peel C. glass D. paper

Ans.

Chapter 8

Disposing of Waste

Do you think about the waste you throw away? Is it mainly biodegradable or not?

 Read the key points below. When you finish, check the box. 

Key Points: Waste Disposal

People have developed various methods to dispose of the large amount of garbage and waste they create. Recycling, burning, and burying are a few examples.

Recycling

Recycling is the best option for disposing of plastic, can, glass, and paper waste materials. While paper products take a few months to break down naturally, plastic and aluminum can take hundreds of years, and glass products may never fully decompose! This is why recycling is key. It can reduce the amount of paper, glass, can, and plastic materials that end up in landfills because these products can be recycled into something we can use again.

Burning

Burning is another way that people get rid of natural waste like paper, tree branches, and grass clippings. Burning waste can help reduce the amount of waste that ends up in landfills because it reduces solid waste to ash that takes up less space. However, burning non-natural waste can release dangerous gases and chemicals into the air. These gases can pollute the air people breathe, so engineers have developed ways to contain the harmful gases and clean the air before it is released.

Burying

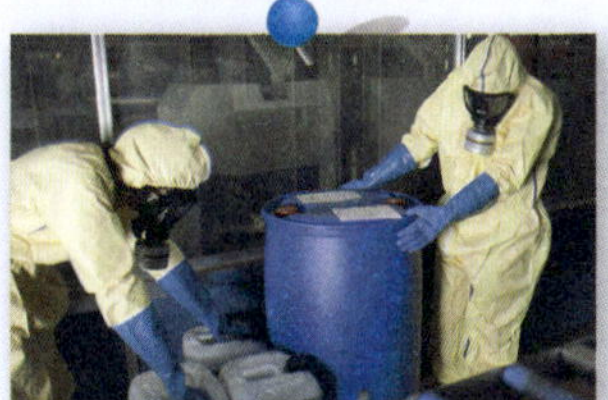

Burying is another method of getting rid of waste. This method is normally used for dangerous and hazardous waste such as radioactive waste. This is the kind of waste that people should not touch or be near, so burying it in sealed containers is one of the safest ways to keep people from coming into contact with it.

 Complete the exercise.

Test your knowledge

Choose the best way to dispose of the following.

A. recycling B. burning C. burying

(1) To dispose of radioactive waste from a chemical plant.

Ans. [ ]

(2) To dispose of 100 cans of soda after a birthday party.

Ans. [ ]

(3) To dispose of tree branches cut from an old tree.

Ans. [ ]

45 Chapter 8
Disposing of Waste

Are landfills a good way to dispose of waste? Can you think of a better way?

Read the key points below. When you finish, check the box.

Key Points: Landfills

Besides recycling, burning, and burying, the most common way people dispose of waste is in **landfills**. Landfills are large pits typically lined with clay, soil and plastic that are filled layer by layer with waste. They were created as a safe way to dispose of waste and garbage so as it breaks down it does not harm the environment and people around it.

Today, some engineers have developed landfills lined with a heavy-duty plastic to prevent dangerous chemicals or decaying materials from leaking into the ground. Besides the plastic lining, every layer of garbage is compressed and covered with a thin topping of soil to prevent air and pests from getting at the garbage.

Although landfills have been designed to be a safe option for waste disposal they can still have issues. Landfills that are not vented properly can cause a dangerous build up of methane, a type of gas that can be harmful to people and the atmosphere. Other issues can occur if liquid waste leaks through the seams in the plastic liner and gets into our ground water. This can contaminate the ground water and make people sick. It can also harm plants and animals in the surrounding area. A last major problem with landfills is that they cannot hold an endless amount of waste. Landfills often become full and need to be closed up. This leads to the creation of more landfills to continue collecting the large amount of garbage people produce.

Gases such as methane generated in landfills are collected by special equipment and pumped through pipes into a storage facility to be used as an energy source.

Complete the exercise.

Test your knowledge

Answer the questions below about the reading.

(1) What is a landfill?

A. a large pit filled layer by layer with garbage
B. a place where waste is collected to be reused
C. a place where waste is sorted
D. a large factory that produces waste

Ans. 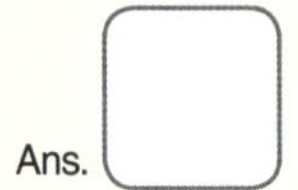

(2) Which is not a possible problem with a landfill?

A. harmful liquid waste leaking into the ground
B. build-up of methane gas
C. helping waste break down faster
D. endangering nearby plants and animals

Ans. 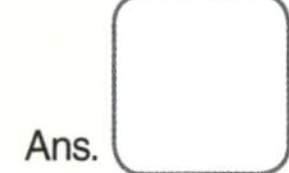

Chapter 8

Disposing of Waste

Use the word box below to fill in the blanks and review key vocabulary.

Review the Key Points

Objects like used paper, discarded food and other things you don't want are called [ ].

Most of the waste or trash humans throw out is not [ ] and will not naturally break down into the soil. Paper, plastic, and glass all take a long time to break down when they are thrown away. They are non-biodegradable, because even when they break down they are not adding nutrients to the earth. When biodegradable and non-biodegradable materials are thrown out together it can slow down the natural break-down of the biodegradable material.

People have developed various methods to dispose of the large amount of garbage and waste they create. Recycling, burning, and burying are a few examples.

Recycling is the best option for disposing of plastic, glass, and paper waste materials. Burning is another way that people get rid of natural waste like paper, tree branches, and grass clippings. [ ] is another method of getting rid of waste. This method is normally used for dangerous and hazardous waste such as radioactive waste.

[ ] are large pits typically lined with clay, soil and plastic that are filled layer by layer with waste. They were created as a safe way to dispose of waste and garbage so as it breaks down it does not harm the environment and people around it.

Although, landfills have been designed to be a safe option for waste disposal they can still have issues.

waste / burying / landfills / biodegradable

Complete the exercise.

Math Mission

Use the chart to answer the questions below about the length of time it takes different materials to decompose or break down in a landfill.

Estimated Decomposition Rates

Material	Time
Paper	2-4 weeks
Leaves	1-3 months
Orange Peel	3-6 months
Milk Carton	5 years
Plastic Bag	10-20 years
Aluminum Can	200-400 years
Plastic 6 Pk Ring	400-500 years
Plastic Bottle	400-500 years
Glass Bottle	500 years- forever?
Styrofoam	never?

(1) How long does it take an orange peel to decompose?

Ans. [ ]

(2) How long would it take a newspaper to decompose?

Ans. [ ]

(3) What would decompose first? An aluminum soda can or a plastic soda bottle?

Ans. [ ]

Chapter 8

Disposing of Waste

Read the mission. Then, answer the following questions to help you with your solution.

The Mission

Waste is a major problem in the US and around the world. While landfills are a good option for disposing of waste, they are not perfect. Landfills can leak, become full, and harm the environment.
Your mission is to design a better method to help solve the waste problem.

Before you design...THINK!

1. Describe the mission in your own words.

2. Brainstorm about a solution. Write your notes in the space below.
   Use the following questions to guide your thinking:

(1) What are the problems with modern landfills? How can you fix these problems with your design?
(2) Can you think of a new way to dispose of waste? What materials could you use?

Chapter 8

Disposing of Waste

Read the mission. Then, draw and evaluate your solution.

The Mission

Waste is a major problem in the US and around the world. While landfills are a good option for disposing of waste, they are not perfect. Landfills can leak, become full, and harm the environment.
Your mission is to design a better method to help solve the waste problem.

Design

Draw or write your solution below.

Evaluate

Evaluate your new landfill or waste disposal system. Do you think it would work? Did you use existing technology or did you create your own waste disposal system?

MEMO

Life Science

Chapter 1 Plant Adaptations

Would a scientist say that a rock has adaptations? Why or why not?

Read the key points. When you finish, check the box.

Key Points: What is an Adaptation?

What do the sharp spines of a cactus, the fuzz on a dandelion, and the stinky smell of a corpse flower have in common? They are all examples of plant adaptations.

An **adaptation** is a trait that helps a living thing survive in its environment. For example, the sharp spines of a cactus prevent the cactus from being eaten by animals. The fuzz on a dandelion helps the plant spread its seeds. Even the powerful odor of the Titan Arum, or corpse flower, helps the species survive. The rotten smell attracts beetles and flies, which pollinate the plant.

cactus

dandelion

Titan Arum

Adaptations are one reason why there are such a wide variety of plants and animals on Earth. Each species of plant or animal has its own set of adaptations.

Complete the exercise.

Test your knowledge

(1) Which of the following is the best definition of an adaptation?

A. It is a skill a living thing develops after birth.
B. It is how a living thing reproduces.
C. It is a trait that helps a living thing survive in its environment.
D. It is the way a living thing interacts with its environment.

Ans.

(2) Which of these traits is least likely to be an adaptation in plants?

A. the spines on a cactus
B. the number of petals a flower has
C. the fuzz on a dandelion
D. the bright color of flowers to attract bees

Ans.

2

Chapter 1

Plant Adaptations

Think about where you live. What kind of plants do you see? Are they all the same?

Read the key points below. When you finish, check the box.

Key Points: Adaptations and the Environment

Adaptations in plants are closely related to their **environment**, the area where a person, animal, or plant lives and grows.

desert

For example, plants in the desert have many small leaves and thorns. This helps them to conserve water because there is almost no rain in the desert. They also have roots that grow near the surface of the soil to absorb rainwater quickly before it evaporates.

rainforest

Plants in the warm and wet environment of the rainforest grow leaves with waxy or shiny coatings that help them repel water. The coating is important because it prevents the leaves from growing mold which is not good for the plants.

tundra

In the very cold and dry tundra, plants grow short and small in order to stay near the warm ground. Small leaves are also best for conserving water in an environment where there is very little rain or snow. These plants often have fuzzy stems to protect them from the cold wind.

Complete the exercise.

Test your knowledge

What characteristics of plants can be seen as adaptations that are specific to the environment they grow in? Choose the correct answer from below.

A: desert B: rainforest C: tundra

(1) small leaves, fuzzy stems

Ans. ☐

(2) many small leaves and thorns, roots near the surface of the soil

Ans. ☐

(3) leaves with waxy or shiny coatings

Ans. ☐

Chapter 1

Plant Adaptations

What are some other plant adaptations you can think of? Do you think all adaptations are visible to people?

Read the key points below. When you finish, check the box.

Key Points: Seed Adaptations

When farmers or gardeners plant seeds, they are careful to plant them in a good spot. The young plants will need sunlight, water, and enough space to grow. But what happens to seeds in the wild, when there isn't anyone to plant them? This is where adaptations come in. Adaptations often allow plant **seeds** to travel and spread out. That way, at least some of the seeds are likely to end up in a good place to grow.

Here are some of the different ways that seeds can travel, thanks to their unique adaptations.

Animals: Plants have developed a few ways to move their seeds long distances with the help of animals. One example is a seed surrounded by a fruit, berry, or nut. When an animal eats the berry, the seeds in it will pass through the animal undigested. Then, they are released in the animal's droppings in another location. Other plants have developed a different way of using animals to move their seeds. Some seed pods have hooks or spines on the outside that get stuck to an animal's fur and are moved to a new location. Sweetgum seeds are an example of this adaptation.

Wind: Seeds of some plants have structures that catch the wind. Each dandelion seed is attached to a structure that works like a parachute. This structure is made up of about 100 tiny, feathery strands which help the seed get carried by the wind. Another example is how the two "wings" on a maple seed cause the falling seed to spin rapidly in the air. This spinning lets the seed travel farther than it would if it dropped straight down from the parent tree.

Exploding seed pod: Some plants have developed seed pods that "explode" when they are touched or when they dry out. This sends seeds shooting far away from the parent plant. Impatiens and geraniums are plants with this type of seed adaptation.

Water: Some plants produce seeds that float in water. Coconuts can travel long distances on the ocean from land to land. Some plants that tend to grow near streams, like foxgloves, also have this adaptation.

Complete the exercise.

Test your knowledge

Determine how the seeds are transported to new places. Choose the correct answer from below.

A: wind B: animals C: exploding pods D: water

(1) walnut

Ans. ☐

(2) impatiens

Ans. ☐

(3) maple tree seeds

Ans. ☐

(4) blackberries

Ans. ☐

(5) cotton

Ans. ☐

(6) coconut

Ans. ☐

4

Chapter 1

Plant Adaptations

Use the word box below to fill in the blanks and review key vocabulary.

Review the Key Points

An [ ] is a trait that helps a living thing survive in its environment. For example, the sharp spines of a cactus prevent the cactus from being eaten by animals. The fuzz on a dandelion helps the plant spread its seeds. Even the powerful odor of the Titan Arum, or corpse flower, helps the species survive. The rotten smell attracts beetles and flies, which pollinate the plant.

Adaptations are one reason why there are such a wide variety of plants and animals on Earth. Each species of plant or animal has its own set of adaptations.

Adaptations in plants are closely related to their [ ], the area where a person, animal, or plant lives and grows.

When farmers or gardeners plant [ ], they are careful to plant them in a good spot. The young plants will need sunlight, water, and enough space to grow. But what happens to seeds in the wild, when there isn't anyone to plant them? This is where adaptations come in. Adaptations often allow plant seeds to travel and spread out. That way, at least some of the seeds are likely to end up in a good place to grow.

Wind, [ ], exploding seed pods, and water are some of the different ways that seeds can travel, thanks to their unique adaptations.

seeds / adaptation / animals / environment

Complete the exercise.

Math Mission

The amount of rainfall in an area can affect what type of adaptations a plant develops. The following graphs show rainfall in Place A and Place B.

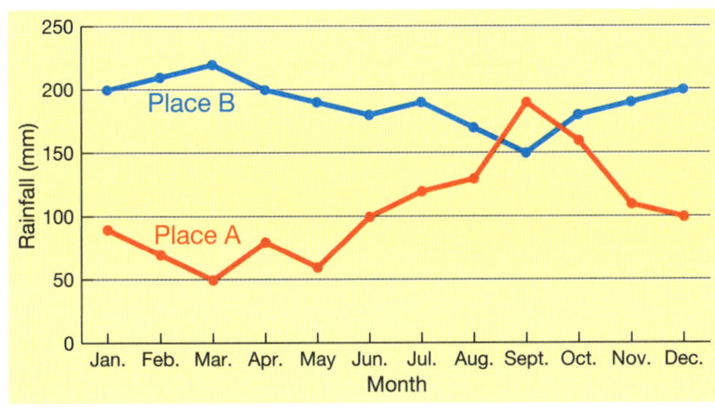

(1) What is the amount of rainfall in March at Place A?

Ans. [ ] mm

(2) Which place has more rainfall in September?

Ans. [ ]

(3) In which place would plants adapted to a rainy environment grow better?

Ans. [ ]

Chapter 1

Plant Adaptations

Read the mission. Then, answer the following questions to help you with your solution.

The Mission

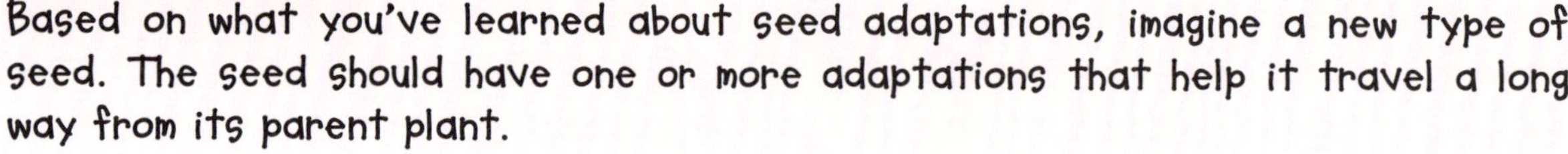

Based on what you've learned about seed adaptations, imagine a new type of seed. The seed should have one or more adaptations that help it travel a long way from its parent plant.

Before you design...THINK!

1. Describe the mission in your own words.

2. Brainstorm your solution. Write your notes in the space below.
   Use the following questions to guide your thinking:

(1) What would your seed use for transportation: wind, animals, water, or some combination of these?

(2) In what kind of environment would your seed grow?

Chapter 1
Plant Adaptations

Read the mission. Then, draw and evaluate your solution.

The Mission

Based on what you've learned about seed adaptations, imagine a new type of seed. The seed should have one or more adaptations that help it travel a long way from its parent plant.

Design

Draw or write about your solution below.

Evaluate

Have you ever seen a seed similar to the seed you imagined? If so, what kind of seed was it? If not, do you think a seed like the one you imagined could actually survive and grow? Why or why not?

7

Chapter 2

Pollination

What is pollination?

 Read the key points. When you finish, check the box. 

Key Points: What is Pollination?

Next time you see bees buzzing around a colorful flower garden, you might want to stop and take a closer look. These bees are hunting for food. The pollen and nectar from flowers are food sources for bees and their hives.

You might wonder why you should care about something as simple as a bee's next meal. It turns out, these buzzing bees have a big effect on you and other living things. That's because as bees are gathering food, they are also helping with an important process called pollination.

Pollination is the process through which plants produce new seeds. During pollination, pollen travels from the stamen of a flower to the pistil on the same or another flower. Without this process plants would not be able to **reproduce**, or make more plants.

Less new plants would create many problems for humans. We would not be able to grow as much food. We would also find ourselves in need of fabrics and the many other products that humans make from plants. There would not be enough new trees to replace fallen ones which means less trees to continue to recycle the air we breathe.

Bees are just one kind of animal that helps with pollination. An animal or insect that helps with pollination is called a **pollinator**. Sometimes pollination happens without a pollinator. No matter how it happens, pollination is something that we all depend on.

 Complete the exercise.

Test your knowledge

(1) What is pollination?

A. When pollen travels from the stamen of a flower to the pistil on the same or another flower.
B. When pollen sticks to a bee or other insect.
C. When a flower blooms.
D. When a bee uses pollen to make honey.

Ans. ☐

(2) What is a pollinator?

A. A part of a flower.
B. An animal or insect that helps with pollination.
C. An animal that eats the whole flower.
D. A flower that only blooms at night.

Ans. ☐

Chapter 2

Pollination

How does pollination create new plants?

Read the key points below. When you finish, check the box.

Key Points: How Pollination Works

Flowers are not just pretty to look at. They are also complex structures. The different parts of a flower play different roles in pollination.

For example, the stamens of a flower produce a powdery material called **pollen**. Pollen grains are tiny and very light. Pollination happens when pollen grains reach another part of the flower called the pistil. Seeds then develop inside the flower—seeds that can someday grow into new plants.

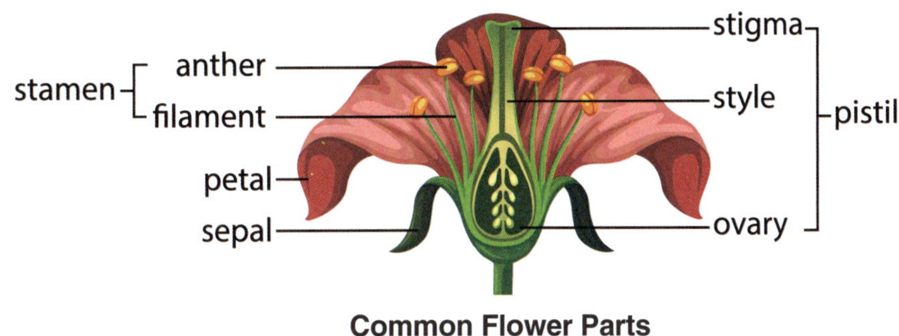

Common Flower Parts

Pollination can happen two different ways. First, when pollen travels from the stamen on a flower to the pistil on the same flower. Or, it can happen when pollen travels between these parts on different flowers with the help of pollinators.

Complete the exercise.

Test your knowledge

(1) What is pollen?

A. a part of a flower that attracts bees

B. a part of the flower that grows seeds

C. a powdery grain particle produced by the stamen

D. a sticky substance that helps flowers grow

Ans. ☐

(2) Which part of the flower produces pollen?

A. the stigma

B. the pistil

C. the petal

D. the stamen

Ans. ☐

9

Chapter 2
Pollination

Do you think pollination happens more often with or without the help of pollinators?

Read the key points below. When you finish, check the box.

Key Points: Types of Pollinators

Insect pollinators like bees can help move pollen to where it needs to go. Of course, animals or insects do not do this on purpose. The pollen just sticks to a pollinator's body when it is gathering food from a flower. The pollen falls off later, pollinating other flowers the animal or insect visits.

Bees make great pollinators because their bodies are covered in tiny hairs that pick up a lot of pollen. Some other examples of pollinators are:

Butterflies: Butterflies have a long tongue that they use to drink nectar from flowers. Pollen sticks to their legs when they are taking a drink and they carry it to other flowers.

Hummingbirds: Long, tube-shaped flowers are pollinated by hummingbirds. The hummingbirds use their long beaks to reach deep inside the flower for nectar. Pollen then sticks to the hummingbird's head. It will carry pollen from one flower to another as it eats.

Bats: Bats often pollinate white or pale flowers that bloom at night. As with hummingbirds, pollen will collect on a bat's head as it feeds. It will then take the pollen to other flowers as it feeds.

Complete the exercise.

Test your knowledge

Match the pollinator with the type of flower it is likely to pollinate.

(1) hummingbird   

(2) bat  

(3) butterfly  

10 Chapter 2

Pollination

Use the word box below to fill in the blanks and review key vocabulary.

Review the Key Points

[ ] is the process through which plants produce new seeds. During pollination, pollen travels from the stamen of a flower to the pistil on the same or another flower. Without this process plants would not be able to reproduce, or make more plants.

An animal or insect that helps with pollination is called a [ ]. Sometimes pollination happens without a pollinator. No matter how it happens, pollination is something that we all depend on.

Flowers are not just pretty to look at. They are also complex structures. The different parts of a flower play different roles in pollination.

For example, the stamens of a flower produce a powdery material called [ ]. Pollen grains are tiny and very light. Pollination happens when pollen grains reach another part of the flower called the pistil. Seeds then develop inside the flower—seeds that can someday grow into new plants.

Insect pollinators like bees can help move pollen to where it needs to go. Of course, animals or insects do not do this on purpose. The pollen just sticks to a pollinator's body when it is gathering food from a flower. The pollen falls off later, pollinating other flowers the animal or insect visits.

pollinator / pollen / pollination

Complete the exercise.

Math Mission

The number of pollinators in an area can affect how much pollination takes place. Fewer pollinators can mean fewer seeds and fewer new plants. Answer the questions about pollinators.

(1) If one bee can pollinate 25 flowers an hour.
How many flowers could 10 bees pollinate in an hour?

Ans. [ ] flowers

(2) One hummingbird can visit 1,000 flowers a day.
How many flowers will a hummingbird visit in 5 days?

Ans. [ ] flowers

(3) If 12 butterflies take 2 hours to pollinate a field of flowers.
How long would it take 4 butterflies to pollinate the same field?

Ans. [ ] hours

Chapter 2

Pollination

Read the mission. Then, answer the following questions to help you with your solution.

The Mission

Imagine you are an apple farmer. You have noticed that there are fewer bees in your apple orchard this year. You usually rely on the bees to pollinate the apple trees so they grow more apples each year. Design a device that can help you pollinate your apple trees.

Before you design...THINK!

1. Describe the mission in your own words.

2. Brainstorm your solution. Write your notes in the space below.
   Use the following questions to guide your thinking:

(1) What traits does a bee have that make it a good pollinator?
(2) What are some traits of other pollinators that could be useful in your design?
(3) What materials could you use to build your device?

12

Chapter 2

Pollination

Read the mission. Then, draw and evaluate your solution.

The Mission

Imagine you are an apple farmer. You have noticed that there are fewer bees in your apple orchard this year. You usually rely on the bees to pollinate the apple trees so they grow more apples each year. Design a device that can help you pollinate your apple trees.

Design

Draw or write about your solution below.

Evaluate

Evaluate your design. What is one thing about your design that could be improved? How might you improve it? Is there a different pollinator you could have looked at for inspiration?

13 Chapter 3 Animal Adaptations

Are plants the only living things that develop adaptations?

Read the key points. When you finish, check the box.

Key Points: Adaptations in Animals

Just like plants, animals can develop **adaptations** that help them survive in their habitat. Adaptations are traits that develop over time. If you look at animals in zoos and parks, you can easily see different types of animal adaptations.

There are two main types of adaptations in animals: one that helps an animal travel through its habitat and one that helps an animal get food in its habitat. This means an animal's body parts will be adapted to help it live in its habitat. As an example, let's focus on the feet of three different animals.

Polar bears have adapted to living on sea ice. Because they live in an extremely cold area, they have fur that grows in between the pads on their feet. These hairs not only prevent them from getting cold, but also give their feet a better grip on the ice.

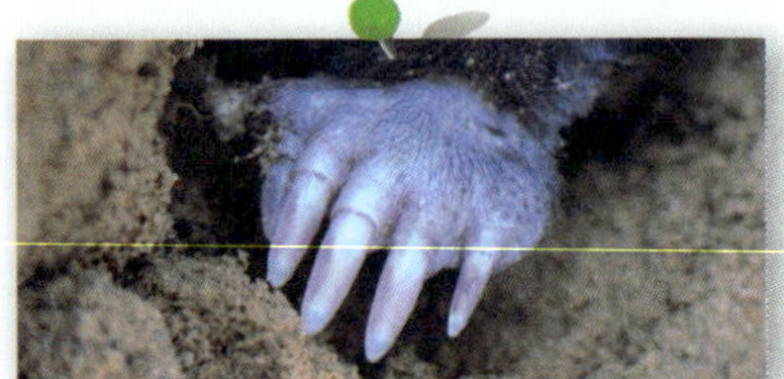

Soil is the best habitat for moles. Soil has a stable humidity and temperature, and worms; a mole's favorite food. Moles can also protect themselves from predators by hiding underground. A mole's paws and claws help them dig tunnels in the soil and move around quickly.

Ducks live near bodies of water, such as rivers and ponds. A duck's feet are large and paddle shaped, so they can easily swim through the water.

Complete the exercise.

Test your knowledge

Match each adaptation to the habitat where each animal lives.

(1) river  ● ● polar bear 

(2) sea ice ● ● mole 

(3) underground  ● ● duck 

Chapter 3
Animal Adaptations

Can you think of other animals whose feet are well adapted to their habitat?

Read the key points below. When you finish, check the box.

Key Points: How Adaptations Happen

Not all differences among living things are adaptations. Some are just that – differences. For example, members of the same plant species might have smooth or rough seeds. Or, members of the same animal species might have different color eyes or fur. These traits are passed from parent to child, even though they might not have a clear impact on an animal's survival.

But sometimes, a particular trait does turn out to be helpful for survival. That is when it can become an adaptation. Here is an example of the process where a trait becomes an adaptation.

1. A bird with an especially strong beak hatches from its egg. This bird has an easier time cracking open seeds to eat than other birds nearby.
2. There is a food shortage. Many of the birds do not survive. But the bird with the strong beak survives because it can get food more easily.
3. The surviving bird has babies. The baby birds inherit the same strong beak trait.
4. The process repeats many times.
5. Over time, the strong beak becomes common in the bird population. The strong beak is an example of an adaptation.

Complete the exercise.

Test your knowledge

Write the letters in the correct order to show how a trait becomes an adaptation.

A. A population of lizards, some that are dark brown and some that are light brown, moves to a new area where the ground is tan and sandy.

B. Light brown lizards reproduce and pass their skin color on to their offspring.

C. The light brown skin becomes an adaptation for the lizards.

D. After several years, there are more light brown lizards and only a few dark brown lizards.

E. More dark brown lizards are eaten than light brown lizards, because they are easier for predators to see on the sandy ground.

15

Chapter 3

Animal Adaptations

What type of adaptation is a bird's beak? Does it help the bird get food or move around in its habitat?

Read the key points below. When you finish, check the box.

Key Points: Adaptations in Birds

Even a single species of animal can have a broad range of varied adaptations. Bird beaks are a great example of this. You can see how bird beaks are suited to many different environments and types of food.

Hummingbirds: Hummingbirds have very long bills, almost like straws, to reach the nectar in flowers.

Herons: Herons and other birds that wade in the water use long, pointed beaks to grab or even stab at small fish or frogs.

Cardinals: Cardinals and birds that eat seeds typically have a strong, cone-shaped beaks, for breaking open seeds.

Hawks: Hawks and other birds of prey have hook-shaped beaks to help them catch and eat small animals.

Complete the exercise.

Test your knowledge

Match the bird to what it eats based on its beak.

(1) fish  ● ● hummingbirds

(2) small animals  ● ● hawks

(3) seeds  ● ● herons

(4) flower nectar  ● ● cardinals

Chapter 3

Animal Adaptations

Use the word box below to fill in the blanks and review key vocabulary.

Review the Key Points

Just like plants, animals can develop [ ] that help them survive in their habitat. Adaptations are traits that develop over time. If you look at animals in zoos and parks, you can easily see different types of animal adaptations.

There are two main types of adaptations in animals: one that helps an animal travel through its habitat and one that helps an animal get [ ] in its habitat. This means an animal's body parts will be adapted to help it live in its habitat.

Not all differences among living things are adaptations. Some are just that – differences. For example, members of the same plant species might have smooth or rough seeds. Or, members of the same animal species might have different color eyes or fur. These traits are passed from parent to [ ], even though they might not have a clear impact on an animal's survival.

Sometimes, a particular trait does turn out to be helpful for survival. That is when it can become an adaptation.

Even a single species of animal can have a broad range of varied adaptations. Bird [ ] are a great example of this. You can see how bird beaks are suited to many different environments and types of food.

food / child / adaptations / beaks

Complete the exercise.

Math Mission

The table on the right shows the results of an experiment to determine how much water, small marshmallows, rubber bands, and toothpicks can be obtained using the four tools which represent a bird's beak in 10 seconds.

Beak type \ Food type	Water	Small marshmallows	Rubber bands	Toothpicks
Scissors	0 ml	4	3	6
Spoon	25 ml	6	12	2
Tweezer	0 ml	2	16	2
Binder clip	0 ml	3	24	10

(1) How many small marshmallows can you get with scissors?

Ans. [ ] marshmallows

(2) How many toothpicks can you get with binder clips?

Ans. [ ] toothpicks

(3) Which tool is the best way to get water?

Ans. [ ]

17

Chapter 3
Animal Adaptations

Read the mission. Then, answer the following questions to help you with your solution.

The Mission

Study the image and text to the right. Use what you've learned about adaptations to imagine an animal that would live in the environment shown in the image. The animal could be one you've seen before, or one from your imagination.

This environment gets a good amount of rain each year. It stays damp and dark, so the ground is soft, muddy, and full of puddles. Other living things in this environment include many small insects, bats, and lizards.

Before you design...THINK!

1. Describe the mission in your own words.

2. Brainstorm your solution. Write your notes in the space below.
   Use the following questions to guide your thinking:

(1) What do you think the weather is like in the location shown?
(2) What kinds of plants do you think would grow in this location?
(3) What kinds of adaptations might help an animal survive in this kind of environment?

Chapter 3

Animal Adaptations

Read the mission. Then, draw and evaluate your solution.

The Mission

Use what you've learned about adaptations to imagine an animal that would live in the environment shown in the image. The animal could be one you've seen before, or one from your imagination.

Design

Draw or write about your solution below.

Evaluate

Review your design. Are there any adaptations you might have also included? Are there any that might be unhelpful to the animal?

19 Chapter 4

Habitat Change

What are some features of your habitat?

Read the key points. When you finish, check the box.

Key Points: What is a Habitat?

Every living thing is suited to a particular environment: its **habitat**. A habitat is the natural home or environment of an animal, plant, or other living thing. A species' habitat includes other kinds of plants and animals that live in the same environment. It also includes things that are not alive such as soil, air, and water.

Changes to a habitat often happen slowly. For example, each year the temperature might rise a little each year or the amount of rainfall might drop.

Sometimes, when a habitat changes, it is not a big deal. Think about when the temperature drops in the winter. Just as you can put on a hat and scarf, other living things have ways of handling the change. For example, mammals often grow thick fur in the winter to help keep them warm. Remember, you learned in Chapters 1 and 3 that plants and animals have the ability to adapt to their habitats.

Complete the exercise.

Test your knowledge

Match the best habitats for the animals in each photo.

(1) deer  ● ● freshwater river habitat

(2) bearded seal  ● ● arctic habitat

(3) catfish  ● ● temperate forest habitat

Chapter 4 Habitat Change

How do you adapt to changes in your habitat?

Read the key points below. When you finish, check the box.

Key Points: Problems with Changing Habitats

As you learned on the previous page, even if a habitat changes, species can sometimes adapt. Sugar maples, the trees that produce maple syrup, are an example of this. These trees grow in the northeastern United States and Canada. Temperatures in this region have been gradually rising, so now the area where these trees grow is shifting further north, where it's cooler.

If changes to a habitat are extreme or happen quickly, plants and animals may not have enough time to adapt. Members of the species might have to move somewhere else, or, over time, they might adapt to the new conditions. If one of these things doesn't happen, the species could be come **extinct** or die out.

For example, after a forest fire, many animals have to go elsewhere to look for food and shelter. The plants and trees they depend on have been damaged or destroyed. The area will generally recover, but it takes time. Some species might not return to the area for many years. In this case, the habitat can recover from the sudden change caused by the fire. But what happens when the changes are too extreme for an area to recover?

Complete the exercise.

Test your knowledge

(1) Which of these conditions would likely cause changes to a species' habitat?

A. the number of trees growing in an area

B. the number of rocks in a area

C. the amount of birds present

D. the amount of rainfall an area gets each year

Ans.

(2) What happens to animals when their habitat changes quickly?

A. The animals always move north to find food and shelter.

B. The animals might move to other places.

C. All animals can adapt quickly to sudden changes.

D. All animals will become extinct.

Ans.

21

Chapter 4

Habitat Change

How do people cause habitat change?

Read the key points below. When you finish, check the box.

Key Points: People and Habitat Change

People can also be the cause of changes to a habitat. One very visible way that humans change habitats is by changing the land. Busy highways are built through meadows. Forests are cut down to make way for houses and other buildings. Dams change the flow of rivers. All of these human actions can change habitats and that can put animal and plant populations in danger.

People are now becoming aware of their impact on the land around them and are taking steps to fix the changes they cause to some habitats.

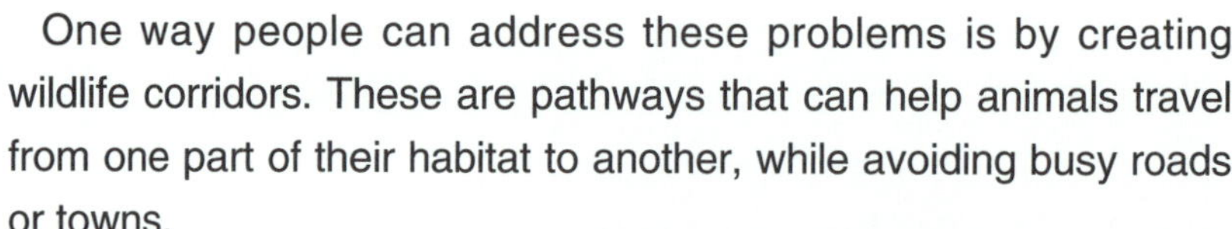

One way people can address these problems is by creating wildlife corridors. These are pathways that can help animals travel from one part of their habitat to another, while avoiding busy roads or towns.

Another possible solution is to change how people design buildings. More buildings could have features that benefit local plants and animals. Once such feature, already being used on some buildings, is a green roof – a rooftop covered in plants. Scientists and engineers are continuing to work on other ideas for making buildings better for local species.

Complete the exercise.

Test your knowledge

Choose one of the best things you can do to prevent people from threatening animal and plant habitats.

A. Build a highway and drive many cars on it.
B. Build dams and change the flow of the river.
C. Cut down trees and build huge buildings.
D. Create a green area covered with plants on the roof of a building.

Ans.

22 Chapter 4 Habitat Change

Use the word box below to fill in the blanks and review key vocabulary.

Review the Key Points

Every living thing is suited to a particular environment: its ______. A habitat is the natural home or environment of an animal, plant, or other living thing.

Changes to a habitat often happen slowly. For example, each year the temperature might rise a little each year or the amount of rainfall might drop.

Even if a habitat changes, species can sometimes ______.

If changes to a habitat are extreme or happen quickly, plants and animals may not have enough time to adapt. Members of the species might have to move somewhere else, or, over time, they might adapt to the new conditions. If one of these things doesn't happen, the species could be come ______ or die out.

______ can also be the cause of changes to a habitat. One very visible way that humans change habitats is by changing the land. Busy highways are built through meadows. Forests are cut down to make way for houses and other buildings. Dams change the flow of rivers. All of these human actions can change habitats and that can put animal and plant populations in danger.

One way people can address these problems is by creating wildlife ______. These are pathways that can help animals travel from one part of their habitat to another, while avoiding busy roads or towns.

people / adapt / habitat / corridors / extinct

Complete the exercise.

Math Mission

There is a forest park A with an area of 4 km^2 and a forest park B with an area three times that of forest park A.

(1) Find the area of forest park B.

Ans. ______ km^2

(2) The area of forest park C is equal to twice the total area of parks A and B. Find the area of the park C.

Ans. ______ km^2

(3) Half of park C was destroyed by a forest fire. Find the area of the half of park C that did not burn.

Ans. ______ km^2

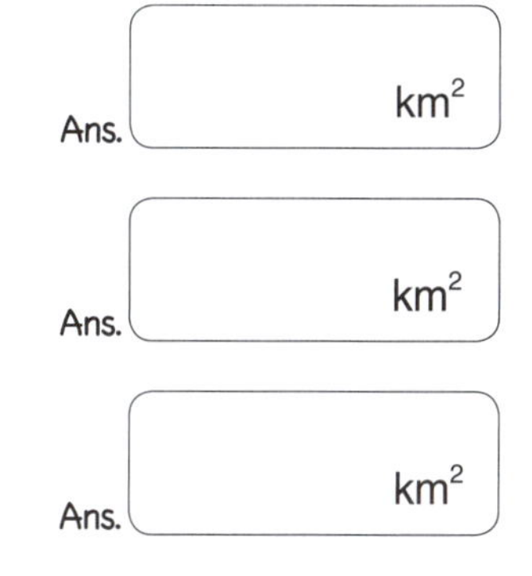

Chapter 4

23 Habitat Change

Read the mission. Then, answer the following questions to help you with your solution.

The Mission

Imagine that you are an architect. Design a school building that does not damage the habitats of local plants and animals. You can plan to build the school near where you live, or anywhere else in the world.

Before you design...THINK!

1. Describe the mission in your own words.

2. Brainstorm your solution. Write your notes in the space below.

   Use the following questions to guide your thinking:

(1) Where will you build your school? What kinds of plants and animals live there? What is their habitat like?

(2) What are some features of your school building that would help preserve local habitats?

24

Chapter 4

Habitat Change

Read the mission. Then, draw and evaluate your solution.

The Mission

Imagine that you are an architect. Design a school building that does not damage the habitats of local plants and animals. You can plan to build the school near where you live, or anywhere else in the world.

Design

Draw or write about your solution below.

Evaluate

Evaluate your design. What challenges might students or teachers have in using your building? How could you improve your design to address those challenges?

Chapter 5

Invasive Species

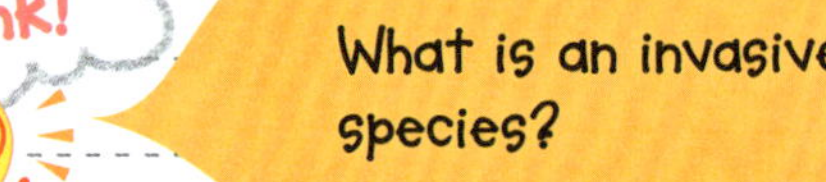

Read the key points. When you finish, check the box.

Key Points: What is an Invasive Species?

Cane toads, like the one shown here, don't have a lot of fans. They are larger than the average toad. Their skin is covered in warts. They eat nearly anything, including small animals. And they're poisonous. Pet owners have to be careful not to let their cat or dog catch one for a snack.

But to make matters worse, cane toads are spreading to new places. As they spread, they are making it harder for other plants and animals to survive.

Cane toads are an example of an **invasive species**. An invasive species is a species that does two things: It spreads to a new area, and it causes problems in that area.

Cane toads were once only found in Central and South America. Then, farmers brought the giant toads to other places such as Australia. The farmers wanted the toads to help eat bugs that were destroying crops.

But the toads reproduced (produced children) and spread faster than anyone expected. Now, the toads are found in much of Australia and other parts of the world. This is causing problems for **native species** in those places. A native species is a species that lives in a specific habitat.

Not all species that are new to an area are invasive. Some traits make a species more likely to be invasive. These traits include:

-It grows quickly.

-It reproduces quickly.

-It has no predators in the new area. (Nothing eats it.)

Complete the exercise.

Test your knowledge

Choose the answer with the correct description of an invasive species.

A. Invasive species are species that have already been living in an area.

B. Invasive species spread to a new area, and they cause problems in that area.

C. Cane toads are now found only in Central and South America.

Ans.

26 Chapter 5

Invasive Species

Can you think of any invasive species in your area? What problems do they cause?

Read the key points below. When you finish, check the box.

Key Points: Examples of Invasive Species

People often bring a species to a new place on purpose, like farmers did with the cane toad. Another example of this is a plant called kudzu that came from Japan to the United States. It was originally planted in the U.S. to help stop soil erosion (the process of soil washing or blowing away). Now, kudzu is an invasive species. Kudzu can grow up to a foot a day which can take nutrients away from native plants that grow around it.

kudzu

Sometimes, people accidentally bring a species to a new area, like the zebra mussel -- an invasive species in the Great Lakes of North America. These small animals were brought to North America on ships from Europe, without anyone realizing it. Zebra mussels are about the size of a fingernail and attach to hard surfaces. They can collect on and cover objects like boat parts, underwater pipes, and the shells of other animals.

zebra mussels

Another way invasive species come to a new area is as pets. This is how the Burmese python ended up becoming a problem in Florida. The snakes were brought from Asia and kept as pets. But, some of them escaped or were let go into the wild. Now, scientists think some native species in Florida are disappearing because pythons are eating them.

Burmese python

Complete the exercise.

Test your knowledge

Choose the appropriate invasive species based on the description of how it came to new areas.

A. kudzu **B. zebra mussels** **C. Burmese python**

(1) A species that was kept as a pet and escaped or was released into new areas by people.

Ans. ☐

(2) A species that was accidentally brought to a new place by people.

Ans. ☐

(3) A species deliberately brought to a new place by people to stop soil erosion.

Ans. ☐

27

Chapter 5
Invasive Species

What can happen to a native species if an invasive species changes its habitat too drastically?

Read the key points below. When you finish, check the box.

Key Points: Problems caused by Invasive Species

Invasive species cause problems for native species in different ways. One way is simply by eating them. In Florida, Burmese pythons are feeding on native foxes and rabbits. The foxes and rabbits can't reproduce fast enough to maintain their population.

Another problem is that invasive species use a lot of resources such as food, water, and space. This means there are less resources available for native species. For example, kudzu grows in thick mats that take up space and block sunlight from reaching native plants.

In Chapter 4, you learned that every species lives in a certain environment, called a habitat. If an environment changes too drastically, native species might not be able to live there anymore. Invasive species can cause these kinds of changes. Zebra mussels, for instance, have caused changes in the amount of oxygen in the water where they live. Some native species cannot live in water with higher oxygen levels and are dying out.

Once an invasive species begins to take over, it can be really hard to get rid of. So, the best protection against invasive species is to make sure they don't arrive in the first place.

Complete the exercise.

Test your knowledge

Match the invasive species with the problems each causes.

(1) kudzu  ●

(2) zebra mussels  ●

(3) Burmese pythons  ●

● They are feeding on native foxes and rabbits.

● Thick mats of them take up space and block sunlight from reaching native plants.

● They have caused changes in the amount of oxygen in the water where they live.

Invasive Species

Use the word box below to fill in the blanks and review key vocabulary.

Review the Key Points

An ______ species is a species that does two things: It spreads to a new area, and it causes problems in that area.

People often bring a species to a new place on purpose. Sometimes, people accidentally bring a species to a new area. Another way invasive species come to a new area is as ______.

Invasive species cause problems for ______ species in different ways. One way is simply by eating them.

Another problem is that invasive species use a lot of resources such as food, water, and space. This means there are less ______ available for native species.

If an environment changes too drastically, native species might not be able to ______ there anymore. Invasive species can cause these kinds of changes.

native / live / resources / pets / invasive

Complete the exercise.

Math Mission

Kudzu is known to grow rapidly; assuming it grows a foot a day, answer the following questions.

(1) If the current length of the kudzu is 10 feet, how long will it be in 7 days?

Ans. ______ feet

(2) How many days will it take for a 5 foot piece of kudzu to grow to 20 feet?

Ans. ______ days

29

Chapter 5

Invasive Species

Read the mission. Then, answer the following questions to help you with your solution.

The Mission

Think about one of the invasive species you learned about in this chapter or you know from your area. Design a plan to stop this invasive species from spreading farther.

For example, you might create a tool to help remove the species from the area. Or, you might plan a system to help people report when and where they see the species to better track it.

Before you design...THINK!

1. Describe the mission in your own words.

2. Brainstorm your solution. Write your notes in the space below.
   Use the following questions to guide your thinking:

(1) What kind of invasive species are you going to focus on?
(2) What are some ways that this species might spread?

Chapter 5

Invasive Species

Read the mission. Then, draw and evaluate your solution.

The Mission

Think about one of the invasive species you learned about in this chapter or you know from your area. Design a plan to stop this invasive species from spreading farther.

Design

Draw or write about your solution below.

Evaluate

Evaluate your plan. What do you like best about your plan? What is one part of your plan that could be improved?

31

Chapter 6

Germs

Have your ever heard of bacteria? Do you know how bacteria can affect your body?

Read the key points. When you finish, check the box.

Key Points: What are germs?

You know that one way to stay healthy is to wash your hands, because it gets rid of **germs** that could cause disease. But what, exactly, are germs?

Most germs are microbes, or tiny living things. They are too small to see with only your eyes. Not all microbes are harmful. There are plenty of microbes around us, and even in our bodies, that don't cause harm or disease. Some of them are even helpful.

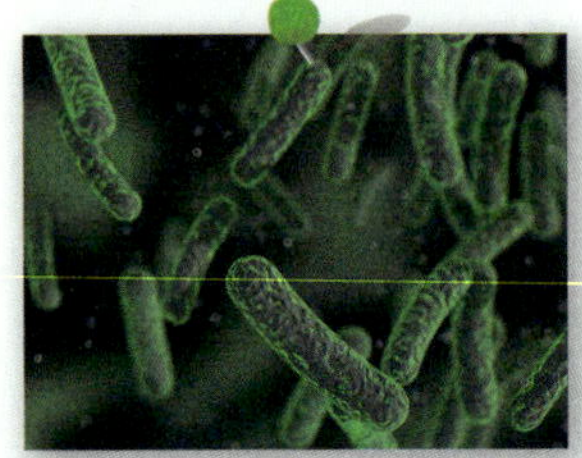

However, for some of these microbes, it's a different story. If germs manage to get into your body, they can grow and reproduce (make more of themselves). They can then produce chemicals that are bad for your body or damage your cells. This can lead to disease. Germs can spread from person to person, which means the disease can spread too.

Germs can enter our bodies in different ways—when you touch your eyes or nose, or through a cut in your skin. But we can do a lot to keep germs away. Washing your hands is one important step. You may have seen a doctor or nurse wearing a mask. That is another way to prevent the spread of germs.

Science teaches us a lot about how germs live and grow. This helps us develop more ways to keep ourselves and our community healthy.

Complete the exercise.

Test your knowledge

(1) What are germs?

A. living things that eat cells

B. microbes or tiny living things

C. cells that live in human bodies

D. large living things that are dangerous

Ans. ☐

(2) How do germs enter the body?

A. through the mouth only

B. through your skin

C. through clothing

D. through openings in the body like the mouth or a cut

Ans. ☐

32

Chapter 6

Germs

What is bacteria? What is a virus? Let's think about the differences between the two.

 Read the key points below. When you finish, check the box. 

Key Points: Types of Germs

■ Most germs belong to one of two groups : **bacteria** or **viruses**.

Bacteria: Bacteria are living things made up of a single cell. This is very different from your body, which is made up of about 30 trillion (30,000,000,000,000) cells! Bacteria cells can be different shapes, including spheres, rods, and spirals.

Some kinds of bacteria cause disease. For example, you may have had a tetanus shot before. A tetanus shot protects you against a kind of bacteria that is found in dirt and soil. It can sometimes get into our bodies through a cut in the skin and make us sick.

Other kinds of bacteria are helpful. We use bacteria to make milk and cheese. You have bacteria living in your stomach that help you digest food. As you'll learn in Chapter 8, bacteria also help break down waste.

Viruses: If you've ever had a cold, you've had a virus in your body. Viruses are very different from bacteria—and from living things in general. Viruses are not made up of cells. They also cannot reproduce on their own. A virus has to use the cells of another living thing to reproduce. For example, when a cold virus infects your body, it takes over some of your cells to make more virus particles.

All germs are small, but viruses are really small. One virus particle is about 100 times smaller than just one bacteria cell.

Like bacteria, viruses are not all bad. Scientists are using some viruses to develop cures for serious diseases.

 Complete the exercise.

Test your knowledge

Answer T for true or F for false.

(1) All bacteria is bad for humans and can cause disease. Ans.

(2) One virus particle is larger than just one bacteria cell. Ans.

(3) Diseases can be caused by both bacteria and viruses. Ans.

33 Chapter 6

Germs

Can you think of ways to protect yourself from germs?

Read the key points below. When you finish, check the box.

Key Points: Getting rid of Germs

■ We can get rid of germs in a lot of different ways. Some methods just clean germs off a surface. Other methods actually kill the germs.

Soap and Water: Normal soap and water doesn't kill germs. When you wash your hands, the soap loosens germs from your hands. Then, rinsing with water washes the germs off. Make sure to wash your hands for 20 seconds!

Chemicals: One way to kill germs is to use a chemical called a disinfectant. Many disinfectants can be dangerous and should only be used by or with an adult. Some common disinfectants are bleach, vinegar, and alcohol. You've probably used hand sanitizers that contain alcohol to kill germs on your hands before.

Heat: Very high temperatures can kill germs. That's why it's important to cook some foods, such as meat, before eating. However, the temperature of hot water you wash your hands in is not hot enough to kill germs. Hospitals often use very hot steam to clean germs from surfaces. Objects that need cleaning are put inside a special machine called a sterilizer. Hot steam is then safely applied inside the machine to kill germs.

UV Light: Some of the light from the sun and other sources is called ultraviolet (or UV) light. UV light can be harmful to your eyes and skin; that's why sunglasses and sunscreen are important when you're outside. However, lamps that produce UV light can be used to kill germs. Drinking water is sometimes treated with UV light to be sure it's safe to drink.

Complete the exercise.

Test your knowledge

Match the descriptions to the methods for getting rid of germs below.

A: soap and water

B: hand sanitizers (contain alcohol)

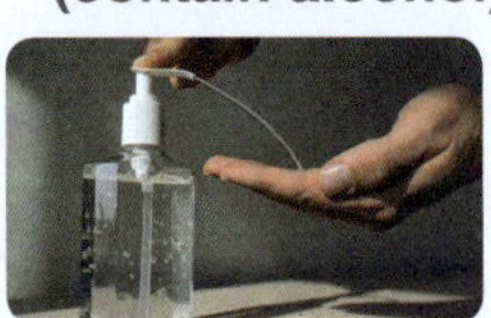

C: sterilizer

D: UV light

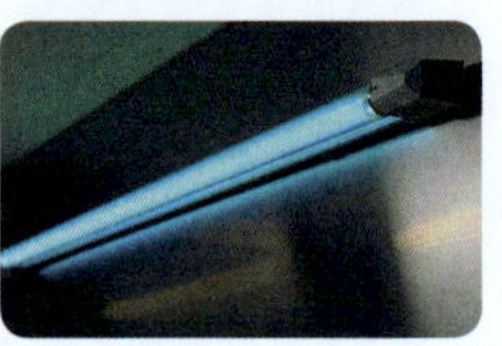

(1) This method kills germs with intense heat. Ans. ☐

(2) This method kills germs with UV light or rays from the sun. Ans. ☐

(3) This method kills germs with chemicals. Ans. ☐

(4) This method rids your hands of germs, but does not kill them. Ans. ☐

34

Chapter 6

Germs

Use the word box below to fill in the blanks and review key vocabulary.

Review the Key Points

Most [ ] are microbes, or tiny living things. They are too small to see with only your eyes. Not all microbes are harmful. There are plenty of microbes around us, and even in our bodies, that don't cause harm or disease. Some of them are even helpful.

Most germs belong to one of two groups : bacteria or viruses.

[ ] are living things made up of a single cell. Bacteria cells can be different shapes, including spheres, rods, and spirals.

Some kinds of bacteria cause disease. Other kinds of bacteria are helpful. Bacteria also help break down waste.

[ ] are very different from bacteria—and from living things in general. Viruses are not made up of cells. They also cannot reproduce on their own. A virus has to use the cells of another living thing to reproduce.

Like bacteria, viruses are not all bad. Scientists are using some viruses to develop cures for serious [ ].

We can get rid of germs in a lot of different ways. Some methods just clean germs off a surface. Other methods actually kill the germs.

viruses / bacteria / diseases / germs

Complete the exercise.

Math Mission

The graph on the right shows how the number of bacteria increases over time. Answer the following questions.

Number of bacteria: 0, 200, 400, 600, 800, 1000, 1200, 1400, 1600

Time (minutes): 20, 40, 60, 80, 100, 120

(1) How many bacteria are alive after 40 minutes?

Ans. [ ]

(2) How many bacteria are alive after 80 minutes?

Ans. [ ]

(3) How long did it take the number of bacteria to reach 1600?

Ans. [ ] minutes

35 Chapter 6

Germs

Read the mission. Then, answer the following questions to help you with your solution.

The Mission

One way people can spread germs from place to place is on their shoes. This can be a problem in doctor's offices and hospitals, where people need to be extra careful about spreading germs. You've probably seen doctors and nurses wearing shoe covers to help solve this problem. But shoe covers have to be thrown away and create trash.

Your mission is to design a device that can quickly remove germs from people's shoes. Imagine your device would be used in hospitals, doctor's offices, and anywhere else where people need to be cautious about germs.

Before you design...THINK!

1. Describe the mission in your own words.

2. Brainstorm your solution. Write your notes in the space below.

   Use the following questions to guide your thinking:

(1) What are some ways to kill germs or stop them from spreading?

(2) What ways of getting rid of germs are safest for people? What ways are more dangerous?

36

Chapter 6
Germs

Read the mission. Then, draw and evaluate your solution.

The Mission

Your mission is to design a device that can quickly remove germs from people's shoes. Imagine your device would be used in hospitals, doctor's offices, and anywhere else where people need to be cautious about germs.

Design

Draw or write about your solution below.

Evaluate

Evaluate your design. What challenges might people have in using your device? How could you improve your design to address those challenges?

37

Chapter 7

How Plants Grow

Plants need soil or dirt to grow. True or false?

Read the key points. When you finish, check the box.

Key Points: How Plants Grow

If you take a look at the lettuce plants growing in this picture, you might notice that something is missing: Dirt. These plants are being grown without soil.

While it may look weird, there's nothing special about these lettuce plants. In facts, most plants can grow without soil.

We are used to seeing plants growing in fields or pots of dirt. But a plant doesn't actually need dirt to survive. Plants mainly need **water**, **sunlight**, and a gas called **carbon dioxide** from the air.

However, just like your body needs vitamins, plants also need a small amount of nutrients. Plants usually get these nutrients from the soil. But they can get them in other ways too.

People often think that when a plant is growing, it's using dirt to grow new leaves, stems, and flowers. But that is not true. The "stuff" that makes up a plant comes mainly from carbon dioxide and water. In some ways, plants seem like magic. They can practically grow out of thin air!

Complete the exercise.

Test your knowledge

(1) What are the main things plants need to live and grow? Choose three from the following.

A. water   B. sunlight
C. soil   D. carbon dioxide

Ans.

(2) Which of the following do plants need just like your body needs vitamins?

A. water   B. flowers
C. nutrients   D. oxygen

Ans.

38 Chapter 7
How Plants Grow

Do you know how plants make their food?

Read the key points below. When you finish, check the box.

Key Points: What is Photosynthesis?

Plants take in water through their roots. But a plant's leaves really hold the secret to how a plant grows.

Leaves capture energy from sunlight. They also take in carbon dioxide. Inside the leaves, the energy from sunlight is used to turn carbon dioxide and water into sugar. This process by which plants use carbon dioxide and sunlight to make sugar is called **photosynthesis**.

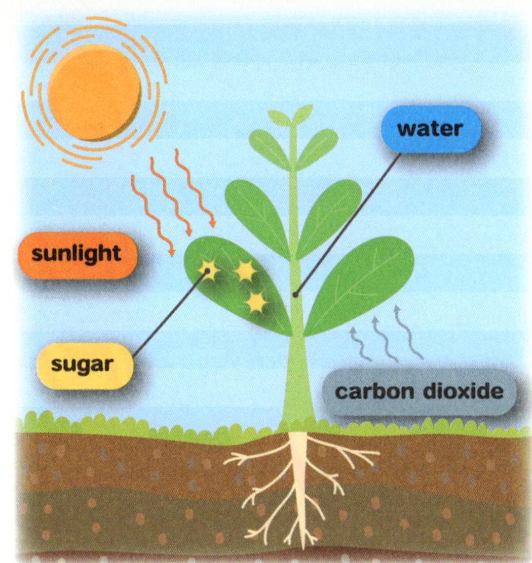

The sugar made by plants is very important. It is the plant's food, or source of energy. It's also a building block for all the parts of the plant—its leaves, stems, and roots. And what about when you eat part of a plant, such as a strawberry, carrot, or bean? What you are eating is made out of the sugars that the plant created.

Plants do need nutrients to survive and be healthy. Some of these nutrients include iron and calcium. Plants take in these nutrients through their roots. Usually, the nutrients come from the soil where the plant is growing. You'll learn more about soil in Chapter 8. But when farmers grow plants without soil, like the lettuce plants at the beginning of this chapter, they can add nutrients to the water. This gives the plants everything they need, without the dirt.

Complete the exercise.

Test your knowledge

Choose one that correctly describes photosynthesis.

A. The process by which plants make sugar using oxygen and sunlight.

B. The process by which plants make sugar using carbon dioxide and sunlight.

C. The process by which plants make sugar using carbon dioxide and water.

D. The process by which animals make sugar using oxygen and sunlight.

Ans.

39 Chapter 7

How Plants Grow

Did you know plants help humans grow? Read more to find out how!

 Read the key points below. When you finish, check the box. 

Key Points: How People and Plants Interact

You have learned that plants need carbon dioxide to make sugar. Where does this carbon dioxide come from? One source of this gas is you! Living things release carbon dioxide. You release it when you breathe out.

The reverse happens when you breathe in. When you inhale, you take in oxygen gas from the air. Where does this oxygen come from? Plants make it when they go through the process of photosynthesis.

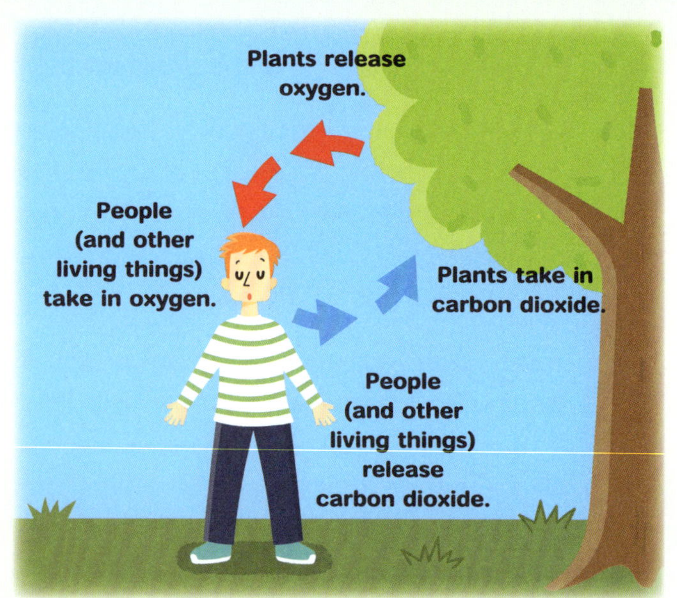

When you look around you, at the air, it's hard to believe that anything is there. You can't see the carbon dioxide gas or the oxygen gas in the air with your eyes. That is one of the amazing things about living things, including ourselves. Living things use materials that we can't even see to live and grow.

Complete the exercise.

Test your knowledge

(1) Where does carbon dioxide come from?

A. non-living things
B. living things
C. the water
D. the soil

Ans.

(2) Which is a product of photosynthesis?

A. air
B. oxygen
C. carbon dioxide
D. water

Ans.

(3) Arrange the photosynthesis steps in order.

A. humans breathe out carbon dioxide
B. plants create sugar
C. plants take in carbon dioxide
D. plants release oxygen

Ans. A → → →

40

Chapter 7

How Plants Grow

Use the word box below to fill in the blanks and review key vocabulary.

Review the Key Points

We are used to seeing plants growing in fields or pots of dirt. But a plant doesn't actually need dirt to survive. Plants mainly need ________, sunlight, and a gas called ________ from the air.

However, just like your body needs vitamins, plants also need a small amount of nutrients. Plants usually get these nutrients from the soil. But they can get them in other ways too.

Leaves capture energy from sunlight. They also take in carbon dioxide. Inside the leaves, the energy from sunlight is used to turn carbon dioxide and water into sugar. This process by which plants use carbon dioxide and sunlight to make sugar is called ________.

The reverse happens when you breathe in. When you inhale, you take in ________ gas from the air. Where does this oxygen come from? Plants make it when they go through the process of photosynthesis.

oxygen / carbon dioxide / water / photosynthesis

Complete the exercise.

Math Mission

You have learned that one of the things that plants need to survive is sunlight.
The table on the right shows the times when the sun rises and sets at three locations A, B, and C on the same day.

	sunrise	sunset
location A	6:45	18:45
location B	6:30	18:50
location C	6:55	19:05

(1) In location A, find the time from sunrise to sunset.

Ans. ________ hours

(2) How much longer is the time from sunrise to sunset in location B compared to location A?

Ans. ________ minutes

(3) Where is the location with the longest time from sunrise to sunset?

Ans. ________

41

Chapter 7

How Plants Grow

Read the mission. Then, answer the following questions to help you with your solution.

The Mission

Many people dream that one day, people will be able to travel long distances through space. One thing standing in the way of that dream is having enough food. We can't bring all the food we would need with us. We would have to grow it.

Your mission is to design a spaceship garden. How would you grow plants on a spaceship? How would you make sure the plants get everything they need?

Before you design...THINK!

1. Describe the mission in your own words.

2. Brainstorm your solution. Write your notes in the space below.
   Use the following questions to guide your thinking:

(1) What do plants need to survive and grow?
(2) How would you meet each of these needs on a spaceship?

Chapter 7

How Plants Grow

Read the mission. Then, draw and evaluate your solution.

The Mission

Your mission is to design a spaceship garden. How would you grow plants on a spaceship? How would you make sure the plants get everything they need?

Design

Draw or write about your solution below.

Evaluate

Evaluate your garden. Do you think it could grow enough food? How could you make it grow even more food? Are you missing any key components for growing plants?

43 Chapter 8
Decomposition

Why are decomposers and decomposition important for the earth?

Read the key points. When you finish, check the box.

Key Points: What is Decomposition?

For most of us, an empty banana peel or brown apple core means that snack time is over. But for a **decomposer**, the meal is just getting started. Decomposers are living things that feed on dead plant and animal parts. Some examples of decomposers are mushrooms, worms, insects, and bacteria. The process that decomposers carry out is called **decomposition**.

When decomposers feed, they break down plant and animal matter into nutrients. This is decomposition. They then release these nutrients back into the environment, so other living things can then use them. For example, some of the nutrients released by decomposers end up in soil. Nutrients in the soil can be used by plants, as you learned in Chapter 7. People often call decomposers "nature's recyclers" because they allow important nutrients to get reused.

We rely on decomposers every day. They help us get rid of waste. This can include food waste, like you read about above. It also includes things like dead and decaying material in forests, and even animal waste. Without decomposers, we'd be surrounded by waste, and plants could not get the nutrients they need to live and grow.

Complete the exercise.

Test your knowledge

(1) What is decomposition?

A. the natural process of plant growth
B. how plants get nutrients to grow
C. the process through which plants reproduce
D. the breakdown of plant and animal matter into nutrients

Ans. ☐

(2) What is a decomposer?

A. a living thing that reproduces slowly
B. a non-living thing that reproduces slowly
C. a living thing that feeds on dead plant and animal parts
D. a non-living thing in the soil

Ans. ☐

Chapter 8 Decomposition

What types of decomposers have you seen at work?

Read the key points below. When you finish, check the box.

Key Points: Types of Decomposers

Decomposers can be found anywhere there is waste material for them to break down. One place you'll always find them is outside. You can find different decomposers in the soil, on trees, or under dead leaves. However, some kinds of decomposers are too small to see with your eyes.

Three major types of decomposers are **earthworms**, **fungi** (or fungus), and **bacteria**.

Earthworms: You've probably flipped over a rock or log and seen an earthworm below it. Earthworms are a kind of animal called an invertebrate. Invertebrates do not have bones. Earthworms eat dead plant or animal material in the soil and release nutrients in their waste, called castings. Castings are a great source of nutrients for growing plants. Earthworms also create tunnels through the soil. This benefits other living things in the soil by helping move air and water around.

Fungi (or Fungus): One familiar kind of fungus are mushrooms. Some mushrooms look a little like plants. But mushrooms don't need sunlight to grow. They get all the energy and nutrients they need from decomposing plants.

Another type of fungi is mold. If you let a loaf of bread sit around for too long, you might notice greenish mold growing on it. The mold is decomposing the bread.

Bacteria: Remember that you read about bacteria in Chapter 6. Some, but not all, bacteria can cause disease. Other kinds of bacteria are helpful. Have you ever taken a deep breath outdoors and noticed that the dirt smells "fresh"? That fresh smell comes from a certain kind of bacteria that breaks down waste material into soil. It's a sign that the nutrient levels in the soil are healthy. Just a spoonful of dirt might contain up to 1 billion (1,000,000,000) bacteria!

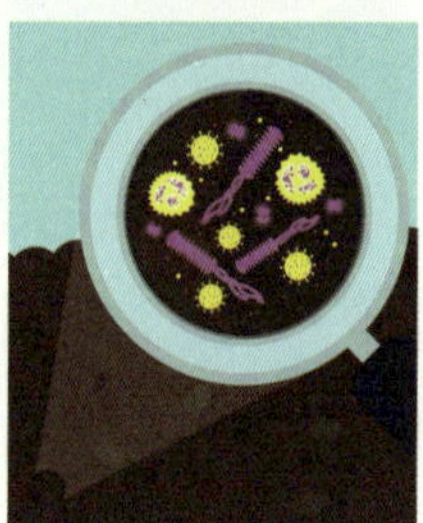

Complete the exercise.

Test your knowledge

Identify the decomposer based on the descriptions below.

A. Earthworms B. Fungi (or Fungus) C. Bacteria

(1) This decomposer is an invertebrate that moves through soil and leaves castings in the soil that provide nutrients for plants. Ans.

(2) This decomposer is too small to be seen by the human eye. It lives in the soil with billions of its friends. Together they breakdown plant and animal waste material into nutrients for the soil. Ans.

(3) This decomposer might look like a plant, but it is not. It gets its food from breaking down waste materials. It also does not need sunlight to grow. It gets all of its energy from decomposing waste materials. Ans.

45 Chapter 8

Decomposition

Do you think people can be decomposers?

Read the key points below. When you finish, check the box.

Key Points: What is Compost?

You probably already know how important it is to recycle. We can recycle materials such as paper, plastics, and metals. Recycled materials are used to make new things so they don't end up as trash.

There is also a way to recycle nutrients from food waste and other materials. This process is called making compost. To make **compost**, you collect certain kinds of waste and let decomposers break it down. Eventually a dirt-like material forms—this is the compost. When you add compost to soil, plants and other living things can use the nutrients in it. In this way, the nutrients get recycled.

Anyone can make compost with enough space and the right materials. The basic steps to follow when making compost are:

Step 1: Collect a mix of natural waste materials (mostly from plants).

Step 2: Add decomposers and make sure they have what they need to live. This includes the right temperature, water, and amount of air.

Step 3: Keep repeating these steps and give the decomposers time to make compost! This can take several months.

Although composting follows the same basic steps, people use different systems. Some people can just create the compost in a pile, or they will use a bin. People might need to mix up the waste, either by hand or by turning the bin to add more air. They can even choose whether or not to add worms to their compost.

Complete the exercise.

Test your knowledge

Choose the best explanation for Composting.

A. the process of collecting waste materials and breaking them down into nutrients
B. the process of recycling plastic or glass into something new
C. the process of preventing soil erosion
D. the process of creating a new habitat for plants

Ans. ☐

46

Chapter 8
Decomposition

Use the word box below to fill in the blanks and review key vocabulary.

Review the Key Points

Decomposers are living things that feed on dead plant and animal parts. Some examples of decomposers are mushrooms, worms, insects, and bacteria.

When decomposers feed, they break down plant and animal matter into nutrients. This is [______]. They then release these nutrients back into the environment, so other living things can then use them.

Decomposers can be found anywhere there is waste material for them to break down. One place you'll always find them is outside. You can find different decomposers in the soil, on trees, or under dead leaves. However, some kinds of decomposers are too small to see with your eyes.

Three major types of decomposers are earthworms, [______] (or fungus), and [______].

There is also a way to recycle nutrients from food waste and other materials. This process is called making compost. To make [______], you collect certain kinds of waste and let decomposers break it down. Eventually a dirt-like material forms—this is the compost. When you add compost to soil, plants and other living things can use the nutrients in it. In this way, the nutrients get recycled.

fungi / decomposition / compost / bacteria

Complete the exercise.

Math Mission

Use the chart to answer the questions about composting.

(1) Find the "Total Amount of Trash" on Day 5.

Ans. [______] gallons

(2) Find the "Total Amount of Trash That Could be Composted" on Day 3.

Ans. [______] gallons

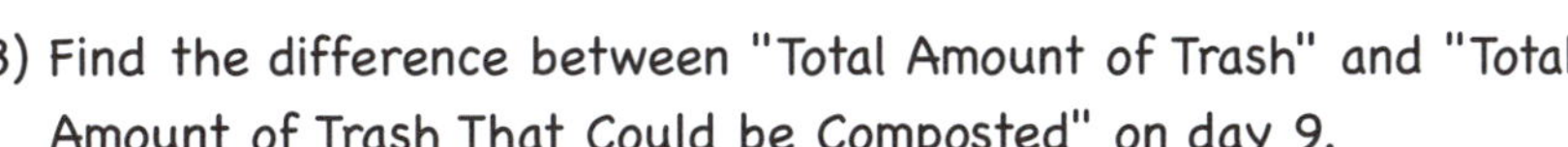

(3) Find the difference between "Total Amount of Trash" and "Total Amount of Trash That Could be Composted" on day 9.

Ans. [______] gallons

47

Chapter 8

Decomposition

Read the mission. Then, answer the following questions to help you with your solution.

The Mission

Design a system for composting food scraps. It can be for your home, your school, or somewhere else in your community. Then, be sure to point out how your system will encourage people to compost.
In other words, for this mission you'll want to think about two things:
1) How compost is made.
2) How to get people to participate.

Before you design...THINK!

1. Describe the mission in your own words.

2. Brainstorm your solution. Write your notes in the space below.
   Use the following questions to guide your thinking:

(1) What are the steps for making compost? What type of decomposers will you use?
(2) Think of some reasons people might not like to compost. How can you make your system better?

48

Chapter 8

Decomposition

Read the mission. Then, draw and evaluate your solution.

The Mission

Design a system for composting food scraps. It can be for home, your school, or somewhere else in your community. Then, be sure to point out how your system will encourage people to compost.

Design

Draw or write about your solution below.

Evaluate

Evaluate your composting system. Would you want to use it? Why or why not?

MEMO

Physical Science

Chapter 1
Forces and Motion

What makes an object move?

Read the key points. When you finish, check the box.

Key Points: What is a force?

A **force** is a push or a pull on an object created by its interaction with another object. Applying force to an object can change its **motion**. For example, if you throw a ball to your friend, you are using a pushing force to make it move toward him or her. When your friend catches the ball, he or she stops the ball's motion.

Examples of how forces make objects move.

push

push

pull

Direction is the path an object takes as it moves. If force is applied to an object, it can change its direction. For example, if an object is moving in a straight line and force is applied to it, the object might change direction. This is what happens when you hit a ping pong ball that is coming toward you with your paddle. You are applying a force to change its direction.

Complete the exercise.

Test your knowledge

Look at where the force is applied to each object and choose the correct direction of motion.

(1) hitting a ball

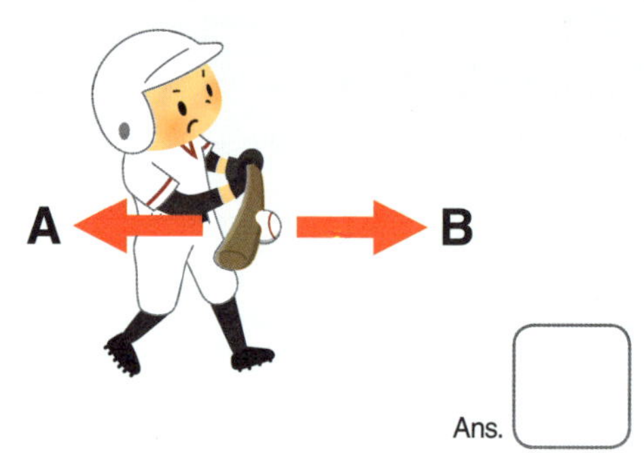

Ans. ☐

(2) opening a door

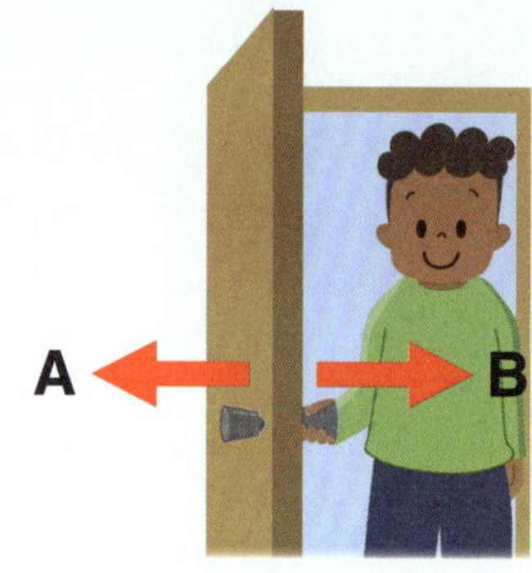

Ans. ☐

Chapter 1
Forces and Motion

Do you think the amount of strength behind a force is important?

Read the key points below. When you finish, check the box.

Key Points: Balanced and Unbalanced Forces

Sometimes more than one force can act on an object. When this happens, the strength and direction of the forces applied to the object will determine if the object moves, and in what direction.

Forces that are equal in strength but opposite in direction are called **balanced forces**. Balanced forces do not cause a change in the motion of an object. When balanced forces act on an object at rest, the object often stays a rest. If balanced forces act on an object in motion, it will continue moving in the same direction and at a constant speed. The key point about balanced forces is that they act with an equal amount of force but in opposite directions.

For example, when two even teams of children pull on a tug-of-war rope with the same amount of force but in opposite directions, the rope will remain evenly spaced between the two teams.

But what happens if one team has more children who can pull the rope with more force? In this case, the rope will move in the direction the stronger team is pulling. When forces are no longer equal, they are considered **unbalanced forces**. Unbalanced forces are not equal. One force is always stronger than the other.

Unbalanced forces change the motion of an object. If an object is at rest and an unbalanced force pushes or pulls the object, it will move. Unbalanced forces can also affect the speed or direction of an object that is already in motion. When two teams of children pull opposite sides of a rope in a tug-of-war the stronger team will always pull the rope with more force, which will cause it to move toward them.

Complete the exercise.

Test your knowledge

(1) Glenn is walking his dog. The dog starts to pull on the leash, so Glenn pulls back with equal force. This makes them both stop moving foward. Is the force on the leash balanced or unbalanced?

Ans. 

(2) Sam and Mike are both pushing from opposite sides of a door. The door will not open. Is the force on the door balanced or unbalanced?

Ans. 

(3) Mila hits a baseball toward center field. Is the force on the ball balanced or unbalanced?

Ans.

Chapter 1

Forces and Motion

Do you think strength is the only factor that can affect balanced and unbalanced forces?

 Read the key points below. When you finish, check the box.

Key Points: Friction

Let's remember that balanced forces acting on an object don't affect the motion of the object. But unbalanced forces do affect an object's motion.

However, this does not mean that once a force is applied to a moving object it will keep moving forever. The object will eventually stop moving due to another force called **friction**.

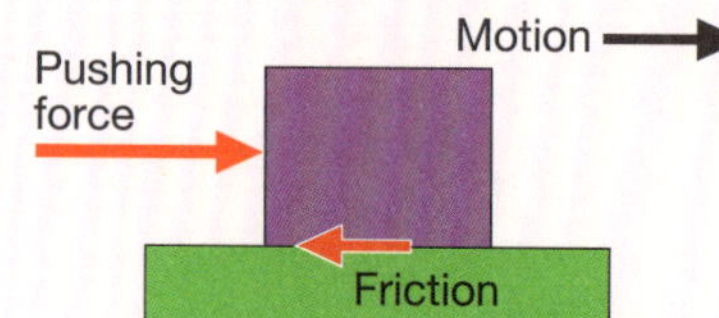

Friction is the force created when two surfaces rub against each other.

The type of surface an object moves against can affect the amount of friction. **Rough** surfaces create more friction than **smooth** surfaces.

For example, when you kick a ball on a field, it slows down because of the friction created as the ball rubs against the grass. Grass is considered a rough surface, so more friction is created as the ball rolls across it. If the ball was kicked on a smooth surface, like a cement parking lot, it would take longer for it to slow down because there is less friction created between the ball and the cement.

What an object is made of is also important in creating friction. This is why metal ice skates glide on ice, but not cement. This is why you go faster down a slide in athletic shorts than if you slide down in jeans. Jeans are a rougher material, so they create more friction against the slide's smooth surface.

 Complete the exercise.

Test your knowledge

(1) Which surface would create more friction against a rolling ball?

A. ice 

B. grass 

C. wood 

D. tile 

Ans. 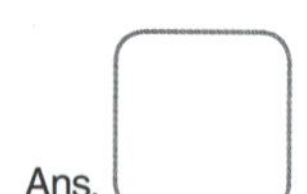

(2) Which type of footwear would help you slide further across a wood floor?
(Hint: Which material would create the least friction against wood?)

 A. socks 

 B. sneakers 

 C. ice skates 

 D. sports cleats 

Ans. 

Chapter 1
Forces and Motion

Use the word box below to fill in the blanks and review key vocabulary.

Review the Key Points

A ________ is a push or a pull on an object created by its interaction with another object. Applying force to an object can change its motion.

________ is the path an object takes as it moves. If force is applied to an object, it can change its direction.

Forces that are equal in strength but opposite in direction are called ________ forces. Balanced forces do not cause a change in the motion of an object. When balanced forces act on an object at rest, the object often stays a rest. If balanced forces act on an object in motion, it will continue moving in the same direction and at a constant speed. The key point about balanced forces is that they act with an equal amount of force but in opposite directions.

When forces are no longer equal, they are considered ________ forces. Unbalanced forces are not equal. One force is always stronger than the other.

Unbalanced forces change the motion of an object. If an object is at rest and an unbalanced force pushes or pulls the object, it will move. Unbalanced forces can also affect the speed or direction of an object that is already in motion.

________ is the force created when two surfaces rub against each other.

The type of surface an object moves against can affect the amount of friction. Rough surfaces create more friction than smooth surfaces.

friction / direction / force / balanced / unbalanced

Complete the exercise.

Math Mission

Different types of surfaces create more or less friction for a moving object. A cardboard ramp was set up to make a toy car roll over different surfaces. Below are the results. Use a ruler to measure the distance the toy car traveled across each type of surface.

(1) A tile floor: ________________________

Ans. ________ cm

(2) A carpet floor: ______________

Ans. ________ cm

(3) A wool blanket: ________

Ans. ________ cm

(4) Based on the results, which surface had the least friction?

Ans. ________

Chapter 1

Forces and Motion

Read the mission. Then, answer the following questions to help you with your solution.

The Mission

You are going to take part in a downhill sled race! You want to win and beat last year's winner. The hill has soft and powdery snow and icy patches of snow. Use the knowledge you have learned in this chapter to design a sled that will help you go down the hill fastest and win the race!

Before you design...THINK!

1. Describe the mission in your own words.

2. Brainstorm a solution. Write your notes in the space below.

   Use the following questions to guide your thinking:

(1) Which type of snow do you think would create the best surface for sliding down the hill?

(2) What materials can you make your sled out of to help you go faster? Wood, metal, plastic?

Chapter 1

Forces and Motion

Read the mission. Then, draw and evaluate your solution.

The Mission

You are going to take part in a downhill sled race! You want to win and beat last year's winner. The hill has soft and powdery snow and icy patches of snow. Use the knowledge you have learned in this chapter to design a sled that will help you go down the hill fastest and win the race!

Design

Draw or write about your solution below.

Evaluate

Did you win the race with the sled you designed? What changes could you make to your sled to make it go faster? Do you think you chose the right type of material for your design?

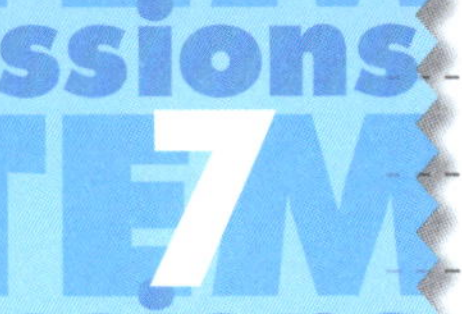

Chapter 2
Simple Machines

Do you know what a simple machine is?

Read the key points. When you finish, check the box.

Key Points: Forces and Work

Let's say you wanted to move a heavy box up a flight of stairs. You might not be able to produce a large enough force to pick it up and carry it. When we talk about the amount of force necessary to pick up and carry a heavy box, we use the word work. When you move an object, this is called **work**.

Let's look at another example. When you throw a ball, force "changes" the motion of the ball. So, work is done. But, when you push against a wall with just your hands, there is "no change" in the motion of the wall. So, work is not being done. Work is done when a force is applied to an object to make it move. If there is no movement, even if force is applied to an object, the action is not considered work.

This means if we want to carry a heavy box up the stairs, we have to do work. But what if the box is just too heavy for us? This is where **simple machines** can help!

A simple machine is a tool made up of few or no moving parts which can change the strength and direction of a force applied to an object. Remember, a force can be a lift, a push, a pull, or anything that makes an object move.

Simple machines make work, like moving things up stairs, a lot easier. When you use a machine to make work easier, it is called **mechanical advantage**. Mechanical advantage is when you need to apply less force to do the same amount of work. If you use a simple machine to increase or change the direction of the force applied to an object, the work becomes easier.

Let's learn more about the types of simple machines!

Complete the exercise.

Test your knowledge

Choose the word that best completes the sentence.

(1) Work means changing the movement of an object by (energy / force).

Ans.

(2) When you pick up a pencil, force changes the motion of the pencil. So work is (done / not done).

Ans.

(3) When you push against a wall, there is no change in the motion of the wall. So work is (done / not done).

Ans.

Chapter 2
Simple Machines

Can you think of a time you used a simple machine to make your life easier?

 Read the key points below. When you finish, check the box. 

Key Points: Types of Simple Machines

The following are types of simple machines.

A **lever** is a straight bar that can move objects without using a lot of force. All levers have three important parts: a fulcrum (that supports the bar), a load (where the bar touches the object and applies force to the object), and the use of force (the force is applied to the bar). A seesaw is an example of a lever.

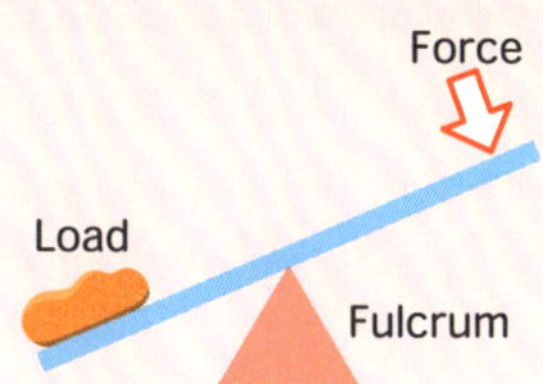

A **wheel and axle** is a simple machine that helps objects move. The wheel has a rod or bar called an axle going through it. Similar to a lever, it changes a small amount of force into a larger force. A wheel and axle is commonly found on a car or a wagon. A ferris wheel, like you would ride at a carnival, is an example of a very large wheel and axle!

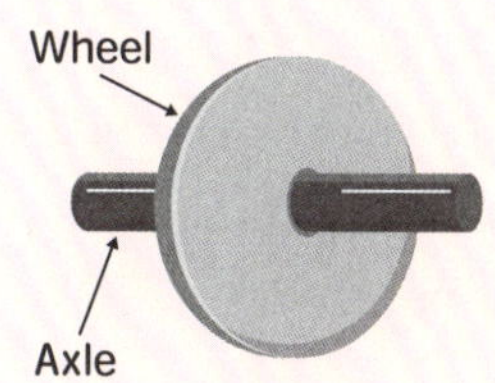

A **pulley** uses rope and wheels to lift or move objects. Pulleys are used in wells to bring water up from underground. Pulleys are also used to raise flags up flagpoles.

 Complete the exercise.

Test your knowledge

Match the type of simple machine to the examples below.

A: lever B: wheel and axle C: pulley

(1) 
ferris wheel

Ans. ☐

(2) 
flagpole

Ans. ☐

(3) 
seesaw

Ans. ☐

Missions 9

Chapter 2
Simple Machines

Can you think of some examples of simple machines in your house?

 Read the key points below. When you finish, check the box.

Key Points: More Simple Machines

Three other examples of simple machines are the wedge, the inclined plane, and the screw.

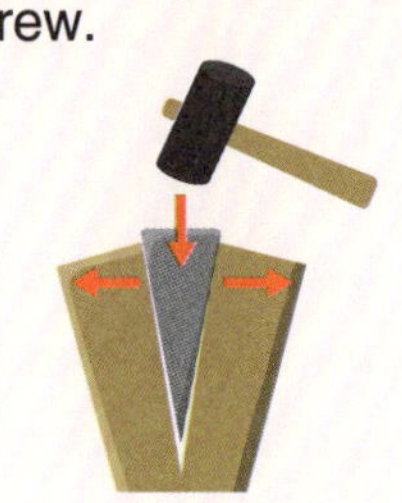

A **wedge** has a thick end that narrows to a pointed end which can be driven into an object to split or separate it. Any force applied to the thick end of a wedge is focused into the thin end, and with enough pressure it will split any weaker material it cuts into. An axe is an example of a wedge. Another example of a wedge is a knife you might use to cut your food.

An **inclined plane** is a ramp that is used to take an object from a lower place to a higher place. An inclined plane can also be used to bring an object from a higher place to a lower place. Inclined planes are often used to move large or heavy objects that cannot be picked up easily. Slides and ramps are good examples of inclined planes.

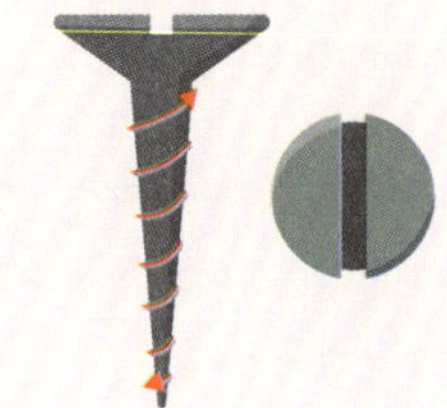

A **screw** has an inclined plane called a thread which is wrapped around an axle. The tip of a screw is often pointed so it can act like a wedge. As you turn the head of a screw, the thread grips into the wood or material you are driving the screw into. This helps hold the material together. Screws are normally used to build objects. Everything from a bookcase to a building can be held together with screws.

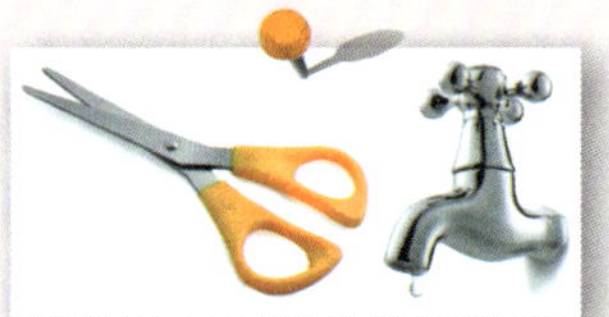

Sometimes two or more simple machines can be combined to create a **compound machine**. For example, scissors are a compound machine that uses a lever and wedge. A water faucet uses a wheel and axle, and a screw.

 Complete the exercise.

Test your knowledge

Use the word in the box to answer the questions.

wedge / inclined plane / screws

(1) A ramp for a wheelchair is an example of an [ ].

Ans.

(2) The axe used to chop down a tree is one example of a [ ].

Ans.

(3) When you make wooden shelves, you use [ ] to join those planks together.

Ans.

Chapter 2
Simple Machines

Use the word box below to fill in the blanks and review key vocabulary.

Review the Key Points

[ ] is done when a force is applied to an object to make it move. If there is no movement, even if force is applied to an object, the action is not considered work.

A [ ] machine is a tool made up of few or no moving parts which can change the strength and direction of a force applied to an object. Remember, a force can be a lift, a push, a pull, or anything that makes an object move.

When you use a machine to make work easier, it is called mechanical advantage. If you use a simple machine to increase or change the direction of the force applied to an object, the work becomes easier.

The following are types of simple machines.

- A [ ] is a straight bar that can move objects without using a lot of force.
- A wheel and axle is a simple machine that helps objects move. Similar to a lever, it changes a small amount of force into a larger force.
- A pulley uses rope and wheels to lift or move objects.
- A [ ] has a thick end that narrows to a pointed end which can be driven into an object to split or separate it.
- An inclined plane is a ramp that is used to take an object from a lower place to a higher place.
- A screw has an inclined plane called a thread which is wrapped around an axle. The tip of a screw is often pointed so it can act like a wedge.

Sometimes two or more simple machines can be combined to create a [ ] machine.

simple / wedge / compound / work / lever

Complete the exercise.

Math Mission

(1) If you used 2 pounds of force to push one side of a lever down, it would help you lift a 10 pound rock. How many pounds of force would you have to use to lift a 30 pound rock?

Ans. [ ] pounds

(2) If you pull on a pulley with 4 pounds of force it can help you lift an 8 pound bucket of water. How many pounds of force would you need to pull with to lift a 40 pound bucket of water?

Ans. [ ] pounds

Chapter 2
Simple Machines

Read the mission. Then, answer the following questions to help you with your solution.

The Mission

You found a big chest in the attic. However, the chest has no keyhole and cannot be opened by hand. Think about how to open this chest with the help of some simple machines!

Before you design...THINK!

1. Describe the mission in your own words.

2. Brainstorm your solution. Write your notes in the space below. Use the following questions to guide your thinking:

(1) What simple machines can you use to help you open the chest?
(2) Would you need two or more simple machines?

Chapter 2 Simple Machines

Read the mission. Then, draw and evaluate your solution.

The Mission

You found a big chest in the attic. However, the chest has no keyhole and cannot be open by hand. Think about how to open this chest with the help of some simple machines!

Design

Draw or write about your solution below.

Evaluate

What simple machines did you use to move and open the chest? Can you think of a simple machine you could've used instead? Would it have been easier or harder?

Chapter 3
Magnets

Is there anything you know about magnets? Try talking with your parents and friends.

Read the key points. When you finish, check the box.

Key Points: Magnets

Have you ever used a magnet to hang a piece of paper up on a refrigerator? Or experimented with magnets in your classroom? Let's learn more about how magnets work!

A **magnet** is an object that attracts metal materials and generates a **magnetic field**. A magnetic field is the space around a magnet where the magnetic forces of an object are measureable. Think about how close you can hold the magnet near the refrigerator before it sticks -- that space is its magnetic field! Magnets are attracted to metals that have magnetic properties. These metals include iron, cobalt, steel, and nickel.

Metals without magnetic properties are not attracted to magnets. These metals include aluminum, brass, copper, and lead. Other non-metal materials such as wood, paper, cotton, or plastic are also considered not magnetic.

Strong magnets can work through non-magnetic materials like paper, cloth, aluminum, or plastic. This is why you can use a magnet to hold a piece of paper on a refrigerator. The magnet is strong enough to work through the paper and stick to the metal of the refrigerator door.

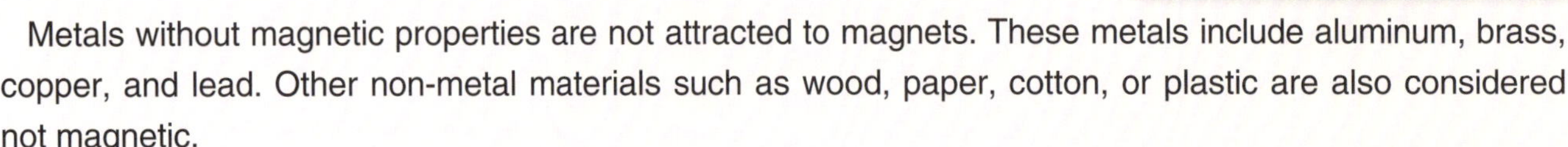

Complete the exercise.

Test your knowledge

Which substance would be attracted to a magnet? Select all correct answers.

A. copper
B. steel
C. wood
D. iron
E. nickel
F. aluminum
G. brass
H. glass

Ans.

Chapter 3

Magnets

Can you think of other magnets in your home?

Read the key points. When you finish, check the box.

Key Points: Magnet Properties

All magnets have a **north pole** (N side) and a **south pole** (S side). The sides of a magnet are named this way because one end of a suspended magnet always points northward while the other points southward. Magnet poles always align with the earth's natural magnetic poles.

Opposite poles or sides attract while same poles repel. When two magnets or a magnet and a metal object attract, they move toward each other. When two magnets repel, they are forced away from each other.

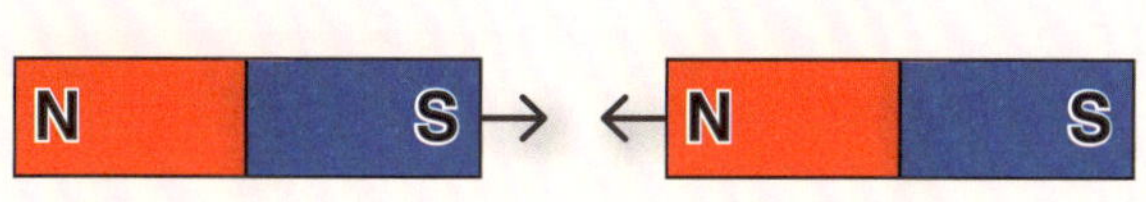

Opposite poles **attract**

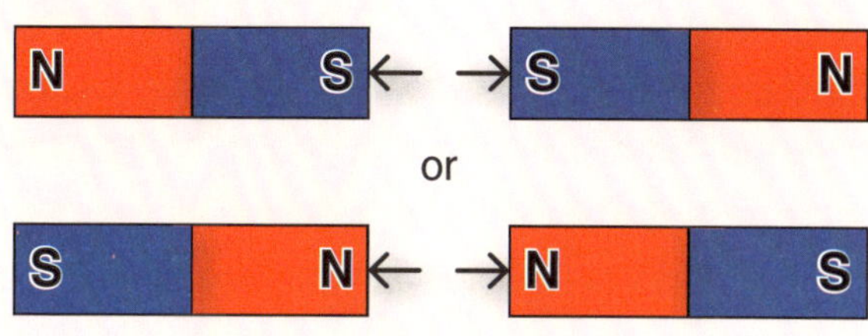

Same poles **repel**

Complete the exercise.

Test your knowledge

Determine if the magnets below will attract or repel each other.

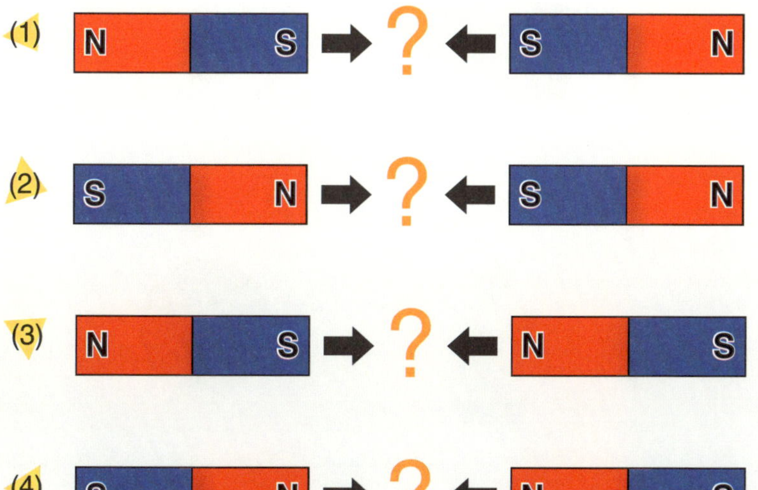

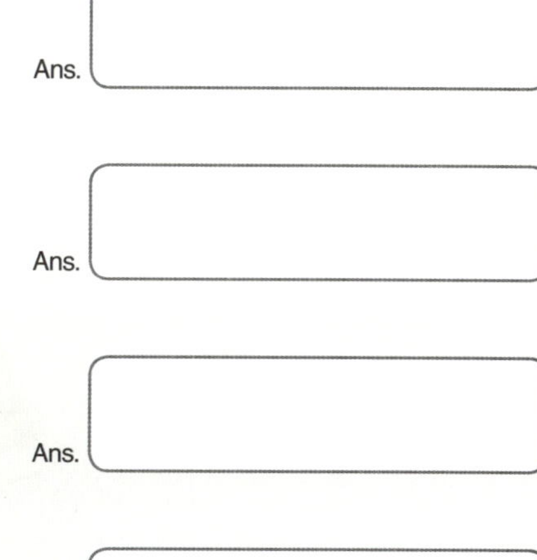

Chapter 3 Magnets

What are some ways people use magnets?

 Read the key points. When you finish, check the box.

Key Points: Uses for Magnets

Magnets are important tools for scientists and engineers. They can help make tasks easier or help solve a problem. Engineers have even developed ways to store information on computers using magnetic memory technology!

Believe it or not, your home contains many magnets you use every day!

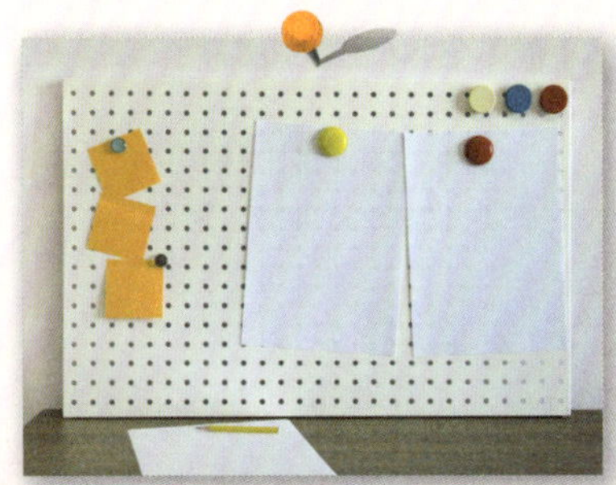

Refrigerator magnets hold papers and other small items to a metal refrigerator door. Other tools like a compass use a magnetic needle to show which way is north. The dark magnetic strip on the back of a credit card stores data in much the same way as a computer's hard drive does. Vacuum cleaners, blenders and washing machines all have electric motors that work by magnetic principles. You'll find magnets in cell phones, doorbells, shower curtain weights, and even some of your toys.

Complete the exercise.

Test your knowledge

Choose all the items that use magnets from the following items found in daily life.

A. vacuum cleaner B. computer C. credit card D. washing machine

E. refrigerator F. cell phone G. blender H. compass

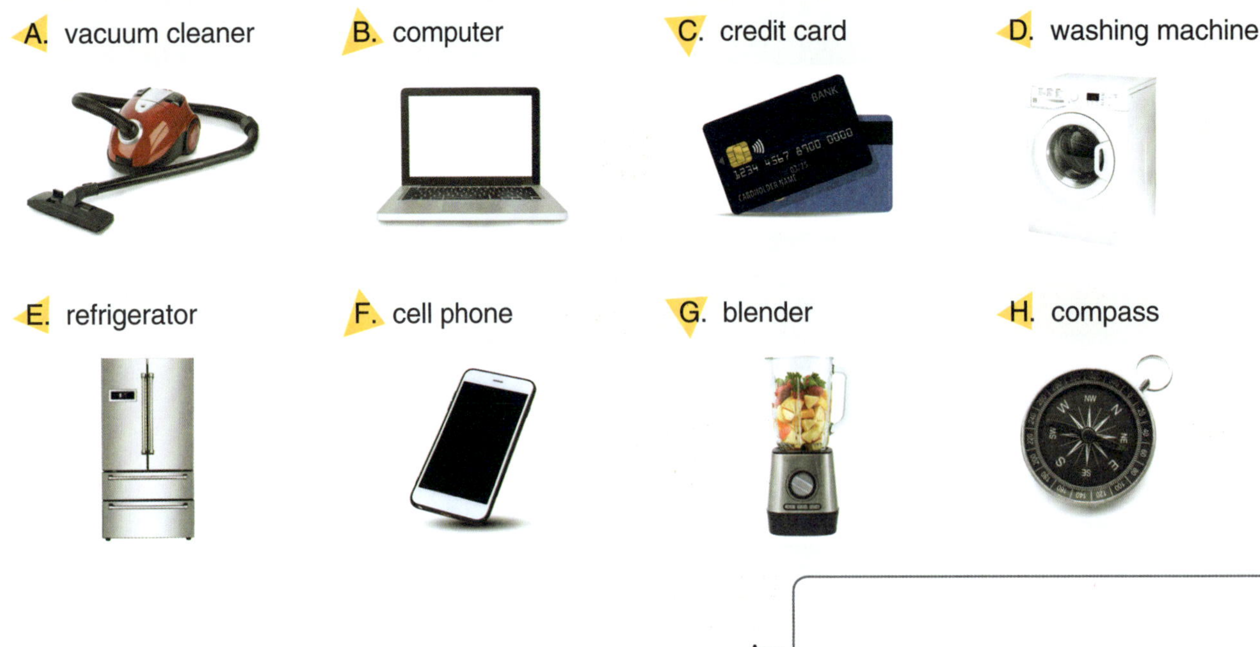

Ans.

Chapter 3

Magnets

Use the word box below to fill in the blanks and review key vocabulary.

Review the Key Points

A magnet is an object that attracts metal materials and generates a [ ]. A magnetic field is the space around a magnet where the magnetic forces of an object are measureable. Think about how close you can hold the magnet near the refrigerator before it sticks -- that space is its magnetic field! Magnets are attracted to [ ] that have magnetic properties. These metals include iron, cobalt, steel, and nickel.

Metals without magnetic properties are not attracted to magnets. These metals include aluminum, brass, copper, and lead. Other non-metal materials such as wood, paper, cotton, or plastic are also considered not magnetic.

All magnets have a [ ] (N side) and a south pole (S side).

Opposite poles or sides attract while same poles repel. When two magnets or a magnet and a metal object attract, they move toward each other. When two magnets repel, they are forced away from each other.

[ ] are important tools for scientists and engineers. They can help make tasks easier or help solve a problem. Engineers have even developed ways to store information on computers using magnetic memory technology!

Believe it or not, your home contains many magnets you use every day!

magnets / magnetic field / north pole / metals

Complete the exercise.

Math Mission

(1) Is it possible to hang a 0.4 lb wallet in a 1.5 lb handbag on a magnetic hook that can withstand up to 2 lbs?

Ans. Yes / No

(2) Is it possible to hang a 0.9 lb folding umbrella and a 0.4 lb key case together on a magnetic hook that can withstand a weight of 1.2 lb?

Ans. Yes / No

Chapter 3

Magnets

Read the mission. Then, answer the following questions to help you with your solution.

The Mission

You accidentally spilled a box of sewing pins on the rug! It will take too long to pick them up one-by-one, and you might prick your fingers! Design a device using a magnet to help you pick up all the pins lost in the rug.

Before you design...THINK!

1. Describe the mission in your own words.

2. Brainstorm your solution. Write your notes in the space below.

   Use the following questions to guide your thinking:

(1) What type of magnet would you use?

(2) How could you pick up the most pins in the least amount of time?

Chapter 3

Magnets

Read the mission. Then, draw and evaluate your solution.

The Mission

You accidentally spilled a box of sewing pins on the rug! It will take too long to pick them up one-by-one, and you might prick your fingers! Design a device using a magnet to help you pick up all the pins lost in the rug.

Design

Draw or write about your solution below.

Evaluate

Did your tool pick up all the pins? How could you improve your tool? Can you add to it or take away a piece from it to make it work better?

Chapter 4

Forms of Energy

What is energy? Where does it come from?

Read the key points. When you finish, check the box.

Key Points: What is Energy?

In Chapter 2, you read about work and how a force is necessary to make work happen. But, did you know that in order to produce a force you need energy? So, what is energy and where does energy come from?

Energy is the ability to do work. Energy makes things change and move. It's everywhere around us and takes many forms. Here are some examples:

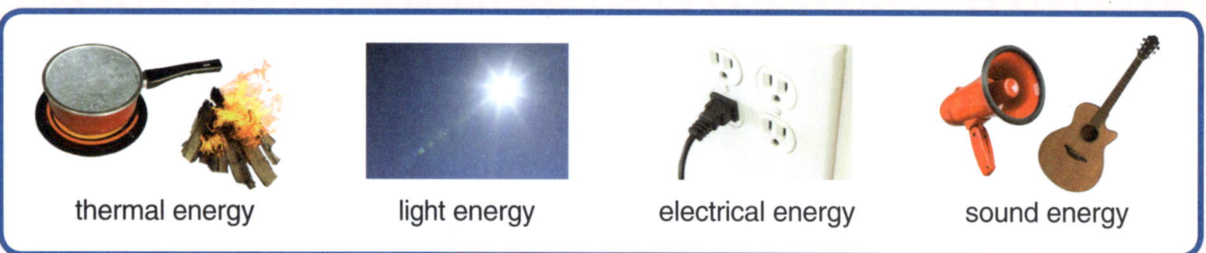

thermal energy | light energy | electrical energy | sound energy

Energy cannot be created from nothing, and it cannot be destroyed. All the energy available in the world already exists! In this way, the energy available to do work always comes from somewhere else, and that energy comes from another form of energy, and then from a previous form of energy before that. For example, when you eat an apple your body takes the chemical energy from the apple and changes it into mechanical energy to help you make your bed or carry out an action. We use the natural properties of energy to turn one form of energy into another, useful form of energy every day. This change from one form of energy to another is called **energy conversion**.

Complete the exercise.

Test your knowledge

Match the form of energy with each example.

(1) light energy

(2) sound energy

(3) thermal energy

Chapter 4

Forms of Energy

Can you think of examples of energy you use in your everyday life?

Read the key points. When you finish, check the box.

Key Points: Heat Energy

Let's explore different types of energy.

Heat energy is a form of energy that is produced by the flow of energy from a warm object to a cooler object. Heat energy or thermal energy can be transferred from one object to another. Energy will flow from the warmer object to the cooler object until both objects reach the same temperature. The transfer, or flow, of energy is caused by the temperature difference between the two objects. **Temperature** is the measure of how hot or cold a substance is.

When energy moves from a warm object to a cooler object it heats the cooler object. The amount of energy used to change the temperature of different objects varies based on what substance they are made of. For example, a concrete sidewalk heats up faster in the summer than the grass next to it. This is because the solid concrete will absorb the sun's rays more quickly than the grass.

Heat also travels between different types of substances. For example, you might use a pot to make hot water on a kitchen stove. When the heat is transferred from the stove to the metal pot, the temperature of the water in it also rises. Once the pot is hot, the water in it will also be hot.

Did you know you can prevent heat from being transferred to other substances? A material that prevents heat from being transferred is called an **insulator**. Cotton, wool, and air are good insulators. Metal is a poor insulator because it is a **conductor** which holds heat easily. So, if you need to pick up a pot of boiling water, please use an insulator like a oven glove or a pot holder, which are typically made of cotton and will protect your hand from the heat.

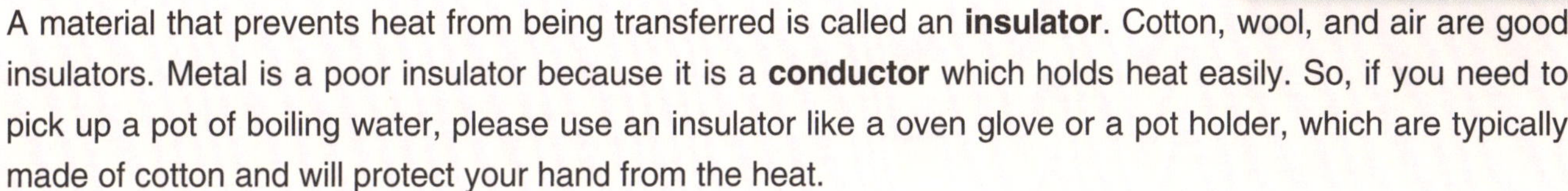

Complete the exercise.

Test your knowledge

Choose all materials that are insulators.

A. wool

B. air

C. metal

D. cotton

Ans.

Chapter 4

Forms of Energy

Did you know light was a form of energy?

Read the key points. When you finish, check the box.

Key Points: Light Energy

Light is another type of energy. Light energy, or radiant energy, is the only type of energy we can see with our eyes. A natural example is the light that comes from the sun and the stars. Although it can be scary, a flash of lightning is also light energy. There are many man-made light sources as well, such as light bulbs and candles. Light energy allows us to fill dark spaces with light, so we can see what is around us.

Light travels in a straight line from its source until it hits an object or surface it cannot penetrate, or pass through. For example, light can pass through glass windows, but not concrete walls. If you enter a room with concrete walls that has no windows or lights, you will not be able to see anything because no light can enter the room. Any material that doesn't allow light to pass through, like concrete, is called **opaque**. Wood, brick, cardboard, and tin are examples of opaque materials.

Sometimes light can hit an object and bounce off its surface instead of passing through it. This phenomenon is called **reflection**. Reflection causes light to change direction or bend. You can see reflection at work if you use a mirror to reflect light from the sun into a dark room or onto another surface. The light shining on the mirror will bounce off its surface and shine wherever you direct it.

Complete the exercise.

Test your knowledge

Answer T for true or F for false.

(1) Light energy is the only type of energy we can see with our eyes. Ans.

(2) Light travels in a curved line from its source until it hits an object or surface it cannot penetrate, or pass through. Ans.

(3) Air is an example of an opaque material. Ans.

(4) Cardboard is an example of an opaque material. Ans.

(5) A mirror is an object that can reflect light. Ans.

Chapter 4

Forms of Energy

Use the word box below to fill in the blanks and review key vocabulary.

Review the Key Points

Energy cannot be created from nothing, and it cannot be destroyed. All the energy available in the world already exists! In this way, the energy available to do work always comes from somewhere else. We use the natural properties of energy to turn one form of energy into another useful form of energy every day. This change from one form of energy to another is called [ ].

Heat energy is a form of energy that is produced by the flow of energy from a warm object to a cooler object. Energy will flow from the warmer object to the cooler object until both objects reach the same [ ]. The transfer, or flow, of energy is caused by the temperature difference between the two objects. Temperature is the measure of how hot or cold a substance is.

Heat also travels between different types of substances. A material that prevents heat from being transferred is called an [ ]. Metal is a poor insulator because it is a conductor which holds heat easily.

Light is another type of energy. Light energy, or radiant energy, is the only type of energy we can see with our eyes. Light energy allows us to fill dark spaces with light, so we can see what is around us.

Light travels in a straight line from its source until it hits an object or surface it cannot penetrate, or pass through. Any material that doesn't allow light to pass through, like concrete, is called [ ].

Sometimes light can hit an object and bounce off its surface instead of passing through it. This phenomenon is called [ ]. Reflection causes light to change direction or bend.

insulator / opaque / energy conversion / reflection / temperature

Complete the exercise.

Math Mission

(1) There is a pot of water on the stove. The pot has been heated to 100 degrees F. The water inside the pot is currently 75 degrees F. How many degrees F does the water need to rise so that it is the same temperature as the pot?

Ans. [ ] degrees

(2) There is a pot of water on the stove. The pot has been heated to 80 degrees F. How many degrees F does the water need to cool so that it is room temperature or 65 degrees F?

Ans. [ ] degrees

(3) If the water in the pot was 60 degrees F, how many degrees would it have to rise to be 108 degrees F?

Ans. [ ] degrees

Chapter 4

Forms of Energy

Read the mission. Then, answer the following questions to help you with your solution.

The Mission

You want to build yourself a house that saves money on electricity costs. Use what you learned in this chapter to create a house that uses natural light from the sun to warm and light up the inside. Keep in mind, your house might get very hot during the day, so you'll also want to have a way to reduce the amount of natural light and heat from the sun entering your house.

Before you design...THINK!

1. Describe the mission in your own words.

2. Brainstorm your solution. Write your notes in the space below.
   Use the following questions to guide your thinking:

(1) What type of material would you build your house out of? Should it conduct heat or let heat out?

(2) How can you direct more sunlight into your house to help make it brighter?

Chapter 4

Forms of Energy

Read the mission. Then, draw and evaluate your solution.

The Mission

You want to build yourself a house that saves money on electricity costs. Use what you learned in this chapter to create a house that uses natural light from the sun to warm and light up the inside. Keep in mind, your house might get very hot during the day, so you'll also want to have a way to reduce the amount of natural light and heat from the sun entering your house.

Design

Draw or write about your solution below.

Evaluate

What knowledge did you use to design your house? Could you have used a better insulator? How could you have brought more light into the room/house?

Chapter 5
Electricity

Where does electricity come from?

 Read the key points. When you finish, check the box.

Key Points: What is Electricity?

Electricity is a type of energy that can make objects move and work. It is used to provide power to lights and all kinds of machines. Like most forms of energy, we cannot see electricity with our eyes, but we know it is there because of what it does. Electricity exists in two forms: **static** electricity that doesn't move and stays in one place until it can be discharged; and **current** electricity, which moves along a path, called a **circuit**.

In order for current electricity to travel through a circuit it needs a **conductor**. A conductor is a wire that holds an electrical current. Conductors are typically made of metal like copper or aluminum. Most metals conduct electricity, but materials like wood, glass, or plastic do not conduct electricity.

So how do we generate a current for the conductor to carry? One way to generate a current is by using **batteries**. You probably know what a battery is and how it is used. You may use batteries to power your video game controller or your calculator for school. But, do you know how a battery works?

A battery is a container that is made up of multiple cells, or compartments, which store chemical energy that can be converted to electricity. When a battery is plugged into a device, the chemical energy inside it is converted to electrical energy as it runs through the circuit. This powers your calculator or turns on your light bulb. If you remove the battery, you break the circuit and the energy is no longer transferred to your device.

 Complete the exercise.

Test your knowledge

(1) What are the two forms of electricity?

A. static and conductor B. static and current
C. current and conductor D. current and energy

Ans.

(2) Which form of electricity stays in one place?

A. static B. current

Ans.

(3) Choose one of the following that conducts electricity.

A. glass B. plastic C. metal D. wood

Ans.

(4) Which is an example of a completed circuit?

A. B. C.

Ans.

Electricity

Electricity can light up our light bulbs, but what other uses do we have for electricity?

Read the key points. When you finish, check the box.

Key Points: Circuits

Circuits are used to power electrical objects, like lights and computers. As long as the battery is plugged in, the current will continue to move through the circuit and power the object.

However, if you introduce a device called a **switch** into the circuit, you can change or stop the flow of electricity. There are many different ways to use switches in a circuit.

For example, let's say you have multiple light bulbs connected to the same circuit. One option is to place all the light bulbs on the same circuit. We call this a **series circuit**. But this isn't the best option as increasing the number of light bulbs connected in series will dim their brightness since they are all using the same power source. Also, if one bulb breaks, the circuit will be disrupted and none of the other bulbs will light up.

Another option is to place the bulbs on separate circuits. This type of circuit is called a **parallel circuit**. Even if more light bulbs are connected in parallel, their brightness is not affected by the other bulbs. However, this type of circuit drains a battery quicker than a series circuit. But one good thing is that if one light bulb breaks, the other light bulbs will not go out. This is because the current flows through other connected circuits and not through a single circuit that passes through each light bulb.

Engineers use circuit maps to help them figure out how many batteries or what type of circuit to use to power a device. Look at the symbols below to see how engineers design circuits.

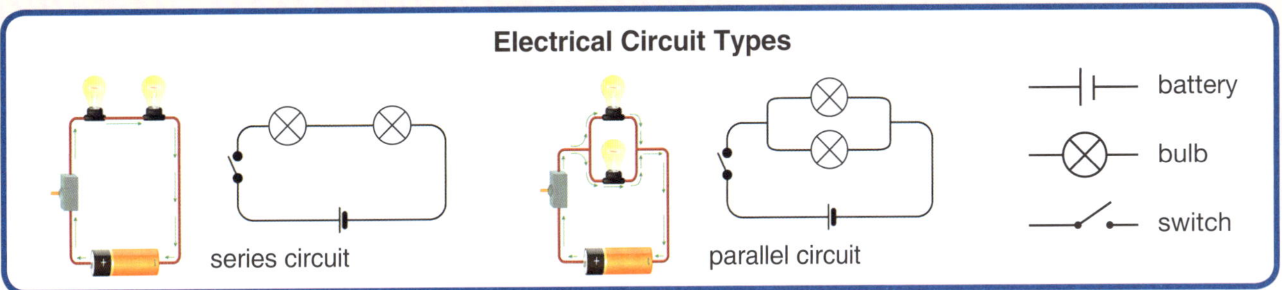

Complete the exercise.

Test your knowledge

Answer T for true or F for false.

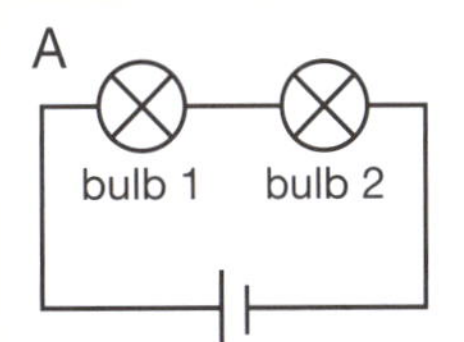

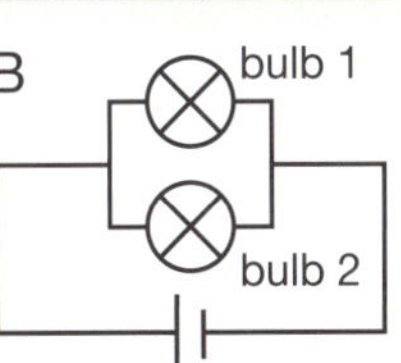

(1) A circuit like Circuit A is called a parallel circuit.

(2) In Circuit A, when bulb 1 is burned out, then bulb 2 does not light.

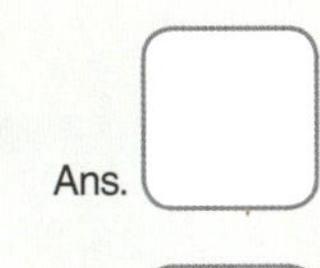

(3) In Circuit B, the brightness of the bulbs I and II will be the same.

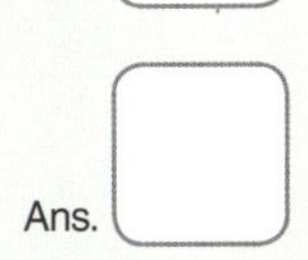

27

Chapter 5

Electricity

Can you think of objects around your home that are powered by electricity?

Read the key points. When you finish, check the box.

Key Points: Circuits and Power

Remember that electricity is a type of energy that travels along a path, called a circuit. When a battery and a light bulb are correctly connected with a wire conductor, the light bulb will light up and brighten the surroundings.

Circuits can be used to power many different types of devices. If you take a circuit that was used to power a light bulb and connect it to an electronic music box, energy will flow through the circuit and the music box motor will create sound. In this way, electrical energy can be converted into other forms of energy (energy conversion).

Forms of energy include light energy, kinetic energy (motion energy), and sound energy. Electricity can also be converted into heat or thermal energy. For example, a hair dryer generates hot air when it is provided with electricity.

Electricity can also be produced by machines. Making electricity is called **power generation**. Most of the electricity we use in our lives is generated in power plants. At a power plant, electricity is produced by turning the shaft of a generator and converting mechanical energy into electrical energy. Electricity can also be forced into a battery through a process called **charging**. A device that collects and stores electricity is called a capacitor.

power plants

capacitor

Complete the exercise.

Test your knowledge

Choose all of the following types of energy that can be converted from electrical energy.

A. light

B. heat

C. sound

D. motion

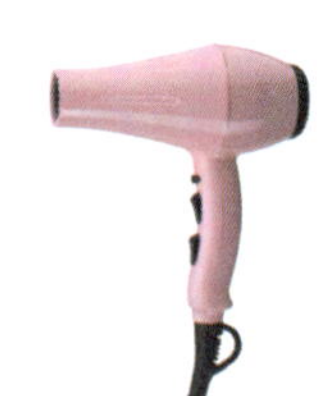

Ans.

Chapter 5 Electricity

Use the word box below to fill in the blanks and review key vocabulary.

Review the Key Points

Electricity is a type of energy that can make objects move and work. Electricity exists in two forms: static electricity that doesn't move and stays in one place until it can be discharged; and current electricity, which moves along a path, called a [ ].

In order for current electricity to travel through a circuit it needs a [ ]. A conductor is a wire that holds an electrical current. Conductors are typically made of metal like copper or aluminum.

One way to generate a current is by using [ ]. As long as the battery is plugged in, the current will continue to move through the circuit and power the object. However, if you introduce a device called a switch into the circuit, you can change or stop the flow of electricity.

One option is to place all the light bulbs on the same circuit. We call this a [ ] circuit. But this isn't the best option as increasing the number of light bulbs connected in series will dim their brightness since they are all using the same power source. Also, if one bulb breaks, the circuit will be disrupted and none of the other bulbs will light up.

Another option is to place the bulbs on separate circuits. This type of circuit is called a [ ] circuit. Even if more light bulbs are connected in parallel, their brightness is not affected by the other bulbs. However, this type of circuit drains a battery quicker than a series circuit. But one good thing is that if one light bulb breaks, the other light bulbs will not go out.

Electrical energy can be converted into other forms of energy (energy conversion).

Electricity can also be produced by machines. Making electricity is called power generation. Electricity can also be forced into a battery through a process called [ ]. A device that collects and stores electricity is called a capacitor.

parallel / circuit / series / conductor / charging / batteries

Complete the exercise.

Math Mission

The chart on the right shows the usable time for each battery.

How many hours does a battery last when used continuously?

Battery	Time
A	7 hours
B	40 hours
C	18 hours
D	2 hours

(1) How many more hours can battery C be used than battery A?

Ans. [ ] hours

(2) What is the difference in usable time between the battery with the longest usable time and the battery with the shortest usable time?

Ans. [ ] hours

29

Chapter 5
Electricity

Read the mission. Then, answer the following questions to help you with your solution.

The Mission

All of the lights in your house are on a series circuit. One day a light bulb breaks and all the lights go out! Design a better way to run the lights in your house.

Before you design...THINK!

1. Describe the mission in your own words.

2. Brainstorm your solution. Write your notes in the space below.
   Use the following questions to guide your thinking:

(1) Do you need to change the type of circuit?
(2) Can you change the type of conductive wire you are using?
(3) Can you add switches or batteries to help balance the flow of electricity?

Chapter 5
Electricity

Read the mission. Then, draw and evaluate your solution.

The Mission

All of the lights in your house are on a series circuit. One day a light bulb breaks and all the lights go out! Design a better way to run the lights in your house.

Design

Draw or write about your solution below.

You can use the circuit map symbols from page 26 to help draw your solution.

Evaluate

Did you use the circuit map symbols to help plan your solution? How could you improve your circuit design? Would you add more light bulbs or batteries?

31

Chapter 6

Sound Waves

How does sound reach our ears?

Read the key points. When you finish, check the box.

Key Points: What are sound waves?

We hear various sounds in everyday life. For example, some people may wake up in the morning to the sound of an alarm clock. We hear the voices of our teachers and friends when they speak in school. We use our ears to capture sound.

Sound is produced when something **vibrates** or moves back and forth through a substance like air or water. Think about how a guitar produces sound. When the player's fingers pluck a string, a vibration is generated and you hear a sound. Another example of sound produced by vibration is your voice. We produce sound from our mouths thanks to a vibrating membrane in our throats called a vocal cord. You can even feel it vibrate if you place your fingers on your throat and hum a song!

These vibrations generate sound energy in the form of **sound waves**. Sound energy cannot be seen with our eyes, but it is audible, which means it can be heard. However, sound waves can only be heard when they travel through air, water, or other substances. Sound waves cannot travel to our ears if there is no matter for them to travel through.

Complete the exercise.

Test your knowledge

Answer T for true or F for false.

(1) A person's voice is one example of sound.

Ans. ☐

(2) Sound is produced by back and forth movement called vibration.

Ans. ☐

(3) Sound waves are waves that can be seen directly by one's own eyes.

Ans. ☐

(4) Sound waves can travel if there is nothing for them to interact with.

Ans. ☐

Chapter 6

Sound Waves

Why are some sounds louder than others? Why are some sounds quieter?

Read the key points. When you finish, check the box.

Key Points: Characteristics of Sound

We can measure various sounds and identify the characteristics of those sounds. Here you will learn some characteristics of sound: "pitch" and "volume".

High frequency | Low frequency
High sound | Low sound

One of the characteristics of sound is **pitch**. The faster the vibration of the object, the higher pitched the sound will be. On the previous page, you learned that sound waves are generated by an object's vibrations.

The number of vibrations for each sound pitch is called **frequency**. A higher frequency value is recognized as a higher pitch. High-pitched sounds have faster frequencies or more vibrations than low-pitched sounds with slow frequencies. A whistle is an example of a high-pitch sound and thunder during a storm is an example of a low-pitch sound.

Another characteristic of sound is **volume**. Volume is when a sound gets louder or softer. As you know, sound is created by vibrations and those vibrations affect the volume of a sound. The greater the vibration, the louder the volume. The smaller the vibration, the lower or softer the volume of the sound.

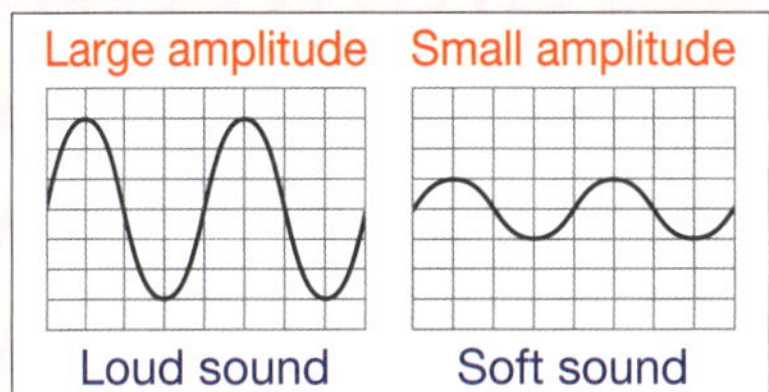

Sounds can also be amplified, or made louder, in several ways. For example, beating a drum with greater force and speed, blowing harder on a recorder, or using more energy when you shout, can all change the loudness or volume of sound.

Complete the exercise.

Test your knowledge

(1) Which wave has the highest frequency? Choose the letter of the best answer.

A.

B.

C.

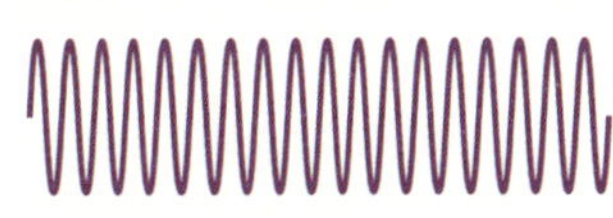

Ans. 

(2) Which wave has the loudest sound? Choose the letter of the best answer.

A.

B.

C.

Ans. 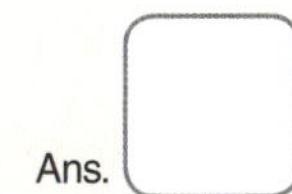

(3) Choose one wrong way to increase the volume of sound.

A. Beating the drums with great force.

B. Blowing the recorder softly.

C. Shouting with more energy.

Ans. ☐

33

Chapter 6

Sound Waves

Are there other ways to change the volume of sounds?

Read the key points. When you finish, check the box.

Key Points: More Characteristics of Sound

Remember that sound waves have to travel through a substance to your ear. And they can travel through different kinds of substances, including things that are solid like metal, liquid like water, or gaseous like air.

When a sound wave hits the surface of an object, some of its energy bounces off the surface. This is called sound **reflection**. If a hard object such as a ball or a stone hits a solid surface like metal or concrete, you will hear a sharp and loud sound.

On the other hand, if the ball hits something soft such as sand or grass, you will hear less of the sound. This is because the energy of the sound wave enters the surface of the object and spreads out. This is called sound **absorption**.

The amount of sound wave energy that is reflected or absorbed depends on the material on the surface of the object. When hitting a hard, smooth material such as metal, much of the energy of the sound wave is reflected.

Another characteristic of sound is **resonance**. Resonance is caused by sound waves that repeatedly hit multiple hard, smooth surfaces at the same time. Have you ever listened to your singing voice reverberating off the walls when you sing in the shower? This is an example of resonance.

A final characteristic of sound is distortion. When you are underwater and you hear someone yelling at you from above the water their voice may sound weird. This is because water disrupts sounds that travel through it. When sound is disrupted as it travels through certain materials, like water, it is called **distortion**.

Complete the exercise.

Test your knowledge

Identify the property of sound based on the descriptions below.

A. reflection B. absorption C. resonance D. distortion

(1) When a sound wave hits the surface of an object and much of its energy enters the surface and is muffled. Ans.

(2) When a sound is disrupted as it travels through matter like water. Ans.

(3) It is created by a sound wave repeatedly hitting the surface of the object. Ans.

(4) When a sound wave hits the surface of an object and much of its energy bounces off the surface. Ans.

Chapter 6

Sound Waves

Use the word box below to fill in the blanks and review key vocabulary.

Review the Key Points

Sound is produced when something [ ] or moves back and forth through a substance like air or water.

These vibrations generate sound energy in the form of [ ]. Sound energy cannot be seen with our eyes, but it is audible, which means it can be heard. However, sound waves can only be heard when they travel through air, water, or other substances. Sound waves cannot travel to our ears if there is no matter for them to travel through.

One of the characteristics of sound is [ ]. The faster the vibration of the object, the higher pitched the sound will be.

The number of vibrations for each sound pitch is called [ ]. A higher frequency value is recognized as a higher pitch. High-pitched sounds have faster frequencies or more vibrations than low-pitched sounds with slow frequencies.

Another characteristic of sound is [ ]. Volume is when a sound gets louder or softer. The greater the vibration, the louder the volume. The smaller the vibration, the lower or softer the volume of the sound.

The amount of sound wave energy that is reflected or absorbed depends on the material on the surface of the object. When hitting a hard, smooth material such as metal, much of the energy of the sound wave is reflected.

Another characteristic of sound is [ ]. Resonance is caused by sound waves that repeatedly hit multiple hard, smooth surfaces at the same time.

volume / vibrates / resonance / frequency / pitch / sound waves

Complete the exercise.

Math Mission

Did you know that sound can travel 340 meters per second through the air? Let's see how fast the sound from certain objects can travel! You can refer to the chart on the right for help with multiplication formulas and answers.

(1) Tom heard the sound two seconds after seeing the fireworks. How far is the place where the fireworks occurred from the place where he stands?

$340 \times 2 =$ Ans. [ ] m

(2) Nancy heard the sound 5 seconds after seeing the lighting flash. How far is the place where the lightning flashed from the place where she stands?

$\times =$ Ans. [ ] m

Multiplication Chart
340 × 1 = 340
340 × 2 = 680
340 × 3 = 1020
340 × 4 = 1360
340 × 5 = 1700

35

Chapter 6

Sound Waves

Read the mission. Then, answer the following questions to help you with your solution.

The Mission

Design an original instrument that can produce various sounds. You want to enjoy a variety of sounds with a single instrument, such as high, low, loud, soft, reverberating, and quickly fading.

Before you design...THINK!

1. Describe the mission in your own words.

2. Brainstorm your solution. Write your notes in the space below.
   Use the following questions to guide your thinking:

(1) What type of material can you use to make your instrument louder? Softer?
(2) How can you amplify the sound from your instrument?

Chapter 6
Sound Waves

Read the mission. Then, draw and evaluate your solution.

The Mission

Design an original instrument that can produce various sounds. You want to enjoy a variety of sounds with a single instrument, such as high, low, loud, soft, reverberating, and quickly fading.

Design

Draw or write about your solution below.

Evaluate

Do you think your instrument was successful in creating multiple types of sound? What part of your instrument could you change to make it work better?

Chapter 7
Structures of Matter

Have you ever thought about what objects are made of?

 Read the key points. When you finish, check the box.

Key Points: What is matter?

Look around the room you are in. What do you see? If you are in a living room, do you see a couch or chair? A rug and a lamp? If you are in your bedroom, do you see a desk? Your bed or closet? Do you see books or video games on your floor?

Now, did you know all those things you can see are made of matter? And if you did know, do you know what matter is?

Let's look at the things around you once again. Each object occupies space in the room. However, a notebook takes up less space in a bedroom than your bed and a couch take up a lot more space in a living room than a lamp. This is because all objects have **volume**. Volume is the amount of space an object occupies or takes up.

In addition to volume, all matter also has **mass**. Mass is the amount of matter in an object or substance. When an object has a large mass, it feels heavy. The opposite is true for a small object. If the object is small, the mass will be light. For example, a notebook is lighter than a desk.

These two characteristics are used to define matter. So, to answer the question above, **matter** is any physical object or substance that has mass and occupies space (volume).

 Complete the exercise.

Test your knowledge

(1) Choose the correct explanation for matter.

A. Volume represents the number of each item.
B. Mass is the amount of space occupied by an object.
C. Every object has a volume and a mass.

Ans. 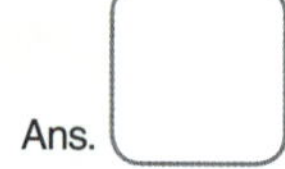

(2) Choose all of the following that are made of matter.

A. computer B. apple C. bicycle D. rock

Ans.

Chapter 7

Structures of Matter

How can you determine how much mass or volume an object has?

Read the key points. When you finish, check the box.

Key Points: Physical Properties

You have learned that an object has volume and mass. But, did you know objects and substances also have other physical properties you can see? **Physical properties** are properties of an object that can be measured or seen without changing the matter it is made up of. Some examples of physical properties are mass, volume, color, smell, and texture.

Physical properties are important because they can help you identify what an object or substance is. Each substance has its own unique set of properties that define it. Let's use the example of the notebook again. What makes your notebook different from your desk?

It is smaller, the pages are white and soft, and the cover is hard. You also know that the notebook is lighter than the desk. These are properties that define the notebook.

Scientists have created many different lists and scales to help us define an object by its physical properties. Let's look at the Mohs Hardness Scale on the right. Scientists use this scale to help determine how hard or soft a rock or mineral is compared to other rocks and minerals.

Mohs Hardness Scale

(Increasing Hardness ↑)

Name	Scale Number	Common Object
Diamond	10	
Corundum	9	⬅ Masonry Drill Bit
Topaz	8	
Quartz	7	⬅ Steel Nail
Orthoclase	6	⬅ Knife
Apatite	5	
Fluorite	4	⬅ Copper Coin
Calcite	3	⬅ Fingernail
Gypsum	2	
Talc	1	

Complete the exercise.

Test your knowledge

Answer T for true or F for false.

(1) Volume and Mass are example of physical properties. Ans. ☐

(2) Physical properties are important because they can help you identify what an object or substance is. Ans. ☐

(3) According to the Mohs Hardness Scale, talc is harder than diamond. Ans. ☐

Chapter 7

Structures of Matter

What other physical properties can you think of?

Read the key points below. When you finish, check the box.

Key Points: Chemical Properties

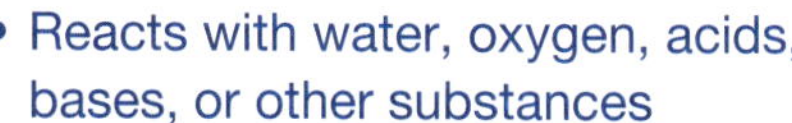

Examples of Chemical Properties

- Ability to rust
- Ability to decompose
- Reacts with water, oxygen, acids, bases, or other substances
- Flammability

Physical properties are not the only properties of matter. All substances also have **chemical properties** that are special to each substance. Chemical properties are the properties of a substance that can be observed when a substance goes through a chemical change. A chemical change is a type of change that also changes the physical properties of a substance.

An example of a chemical change you may have seen before is when metal rusts. Have your ever left your bike out in the rain or snow for a few days? When you go to ride it again you may have seen an orange-red colored material built-up on the bike chain. This is rust. Rust is the result of a chemical reaction between the metal of your bike and precipitation like rain or snow. And once metal rusts you cannot change it back. This is what makes rust a chemical change.

So why do substances have chemical properties? To answer that you must look at what a substance is made up of. Everything around you is made up of tiny particles you can't see. These particles are called **atoms**.

Atoms are the building blocks for substances called **elements**. Elements have specific chemical and physical properties that cannot be broken down into other substances through ordinary chemical reactions. All substances in the world are made of elements. Examples of elements include hydrogen, oxygen, aluminum, calcium, and iron. There are more than 120 elements!

Elements react differently when they encounter other elements. For example, your bike rusts because it is made of iron and the physical properties of iron change when it meets with water and oxygen. These three substances react when they come together to change the physical properties of the bike and form rust.

Complete the exercise.

Test your knowledge

Match the terms below to the correct definition.

A. chemical properties B. atoms C. elements

(1) These have specific chemical and physical properties that cannot be broken down into other substances through ordinary chemical reactions. All substances in the world are made of these. Ans. ☐

(2) These are made up of tiny particles you can't see. These are the building blocks for substances called elements. Ans. ☐

(3) These are the properties of a substance that can be observed when a substance goes through a chemical change. Ans. ☐

40

Chapter 7
Structures of Matter

Use the word box below to fill in the blanks and review key vocabulary.

Review the Key Points

All objects have [ ]. Volume is the amount of space an object occupies or takes up.

In addition to volume, all matter also has [ ]. Mass is the amount of matter in an object or substance.

[ ] properties are properties of an object that can be measured or seen without changing the matter it is made up of. Physical properties are important because they can help you identify what an object or substance is. Each substance has its own unique set of properties that define it.

Scientists have created many different lists and scales to help us define an object by its physical properties.

All substances also have [ ] properties that are special to each substance. Chemical properties are the properties of a substance that can be observed when a substance goes through a chemical change. A chemical change is a type of change that also changes the physical properties of a substance.

Everything around you is made up of tiny particles you can't see. These particles are called [ ].

Atoms are the building blocks for substances called [ ]. Elements have specific chemical and physical properties that cannot be broken down into other substances through ordinary chemical reactions. All substances in the world are made of elements. Elements react differently when they encounter other elements.

mass / atoms / volume / elements / chemical / physical

Complete the exercise.

Math Mission

Scientists can measure different properties of objects. One physical property they often measure is weight. Read the scales below and record the weight.

(1) 0 1 kg, 200g, 400g, 600g, 800g

Ans. 200 g

(2) 0 1 kg, 200g, 400g, 600g, 800g

Ans. [ ] g

(3) 0 1 kg, 200g, 400g, 600g, 800g

Ans. [ ] g

41

Chapter 7

Structures of Matter

Read the mission. Then, answer the following questions to help you with your solution.

The Mission

As a scientist, you have successfully produced a new substance in the lab! Use what you have learned about the properties of matter to describe your substance and define its characteristics, so others will be able to identify it in the future.

Before you design...THINK!

1. Describe the mission in your own words.

2. Brainstorm your solution. Write your notes in the space below.

   Use the following questions to guide your thinking:

(1) What will you name your substance?

(2) What color is it? What is its mass? What is its volume? Is it magnetic?

(3) What chemical properties could it have? Does it dissolve in water? Or rust in the rain?

Chapter 7

Structures of Matter

Read the mission. Then, draw and evaluate your solution.

The Mission

As a scientist, you have successfully produced a new substance in the lab! Use what you have learned about the properties of matter to describe your substance and define its characteristics so others will be able to identify it in the future.

Design

Draw or write about your solution below.

Evaluate

What substance did you create? Did you give your substance physical and chemical properties? How would your substance react with other substances?

Chapter 8
Changes in States of Matter

Can you name the three main states of matter?

Read the key points. When you finish, check the box.

Key Points: States of Matter

Most substances on Earth can be classified as either a **solid**, a **liquid**, or a **gas**. These are the three primary states of matter. Let's look at the characteristics of solids, liquids, and gases.

A **solid** is a substance with a defined shape and volume. The atoms in a solid stick together in a specific pattern and do not move very much. Solids don't change shape unless great force or heat is applied to them. Examples of solids are ice, wood, bricks, apples, notebooks and many other objects.

A **liquid** is a substance that has a defined volume but no defined shape. The atoms in a liquid are less tightly packed than in a solid, but still close together. They can move a little bit because they have more space between their atoms than solids. That is why liquids can change shape. For example, when you pour juice into different size glasses, the juice will fit the shape of each glass. Some examples of liquids are water, juice, soda, coffee, and tea.

A **gas** is a substance that does not have a defined shape or volume. The atoms of a gas are spread apart from each other and do not stick together like in a solid. They do not have a fixed shape because they move around, and the pattern and volume of the arrangement of each atom is not concrete. Some examples of gases are air, steam, oxygen, and carbon dioxide.

Complete the exercise.

Test your knowledge

Match the states of matter to each example.

Chapter 8
Changes in States of Matter

How does matter change form?

Read the key points. When you finish, check the box.

Key Points: Properties of States of Matter

Remember there are three main states of matter: solid, liquid, and gas. Here you will learn that some substances can change from one state of matter to another when energy is added or taken away.

The best substance to use when looking at how states of matter can change is water. Water can exist on Earth in all three states of matter as a solid, a liquid, and a gas.

You know that water is liquid. What happens if you heat the water? As the water warms, the temperature rises. When the temperature of the water reaches around 100 degrees Celsius (212 degrees Fahrenheit), bubbles are produced from the water. This action is called **boiling**. The bubbles that rise to the surface when the water boils are water in the form of a gas called water vapor. The process of water turning into water vapor is called **evaporation**. When water is heated, it evaporates and transforms from liquid to gas.

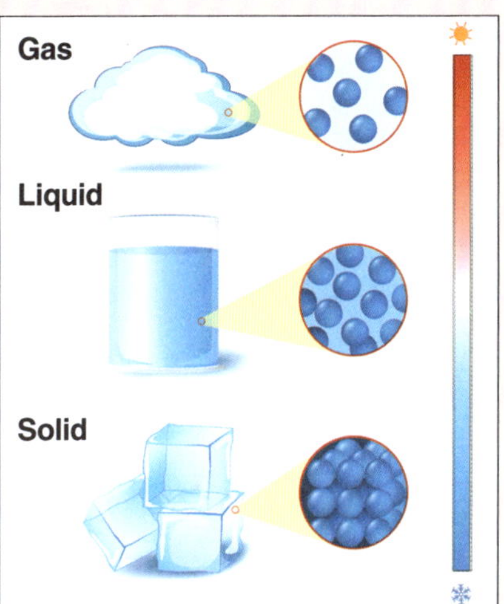

Water can also be cooled. Cooling water will lower its temperature. When the temperature drops to 0 degrees Celsius (32 degrees Fahrenheit), the water turns into ice. You have already learned that ice is a solid. When water is cooled, it changes its form from liquid to solid.

So, water can be a solid (ice), a liquid (water), and a gas (water vapor) depending on the temperature. In addition to water, there are other substances that change form depending on the temperature. For example, the solid wax of a candle melts from the heat of its flame and becomes a liquid wax.

Complete the exercise.

Test your knowledge

Choose the best word to complete each sentence.

(1) If water is kept heated, it will boil at about (0 / 100) degrees Celsius.

Ans.

(2) Liquid water turns into a (solid / gas) called water vapor as it continues to be heated.

Ans.

(3) Liquid water turns into (solid / gas) ice as it cools.

Ans.

(4) The state of matter of water can change from a solid, a liquid or a gas depending on (temperature / amount).

Ans.

Chapter 8
45 Changes in States of Matter

When a substance changes from one form of matter to another, do its properties also change?

Read the key points. When you finish, check the box.

Key Points: Properties of Matter Continued

Remember that all matter has a volume and a mass. You also learned that the state of matter (solid, liquid, gas) can change as the temperature changes.

When a substance changes states, it also changes volume. Substances often increase in volume when they are warmed and decrease when cooled. For example, if a container full of air is warmed, the container will expand because the atoms in the air move faster. The opposite happens if you cool a container full of air. The atoms that make up the air will slow down and the container may collapse in on itself a little. This means that the volume increases when the gas is warmed and decreases when the air is cooled. In this case, we can see the change in the volume of air with our eyes.

If we only use the example of air, you can say that the volume of a substance increases as it changes states. However, water does not follow this rule. When water changes from a solid to a liquid, its volume decreases. In other words, ice has a larger volume than liquid water. Want to see this idea in action for yourself? Try filling a plastic cup with water and put it into the freezer. As it freezes you can see how the ice swells and rises in the glass. When water changes from a liquid to a solid, the volume increases.

Even as the state of matter changes, the mass does not change. Whether the water is warmed or cooled, the number of atoms in it does not increase or decrease. The atoms simply speed up or slow down. So, the mass of a substance always stays the same.

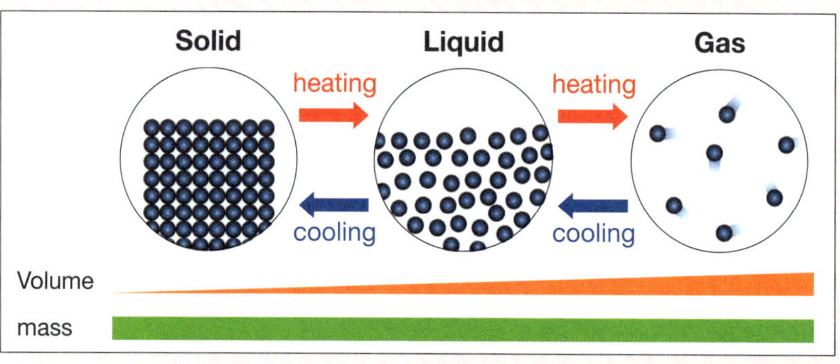

Complete the exercise.

Test your knowledge

Choose the word that best complete the sentence.

(1) When a gas is warmed, the volume will (increase / decrease / not change).

Ans.

(2) When solid ice changes into liquid water, the volume will (increase / decrease / not change).

Ans.

(3) When water is cooled, the mass will (increase / decrease / not change).

Ans.

Chapter 8

Changes in States of Matter

Use the word box below to fill in the blanks and review key vocabulary.

Review the Key Points

Most substances on Earth can be classified as either a solid, a liquid, or a gas.

A [ ] is a substance with a defined shape and volume. The atoms in a solid stick together in a specific pattern and do not move very much.

A [ ] is a substance that has a defined volume but no defined shape. The atoms in a liquid are less tightly packed than in a solid, but still close together. They can move a little bit because they have more space between their atoms than solids.

A [ ] is a substance that does not have a defined shape or volume. The atoms of a gas are spread apart from each other and do not stick together like in a solid. They do not have a fixed shape because they move around, and the pattern and volume of the arrangement of each atom is not concrete.

When water is heated, it [ ] and transforms from liquid to gas. When water is cooled, it changes its form from liquid to solid.

Water can change into solid (ice), liquid (water), and gas (water vapor) depending on the temperature. In addition to water, there are other substances that change form depending on the temperature.
As the substance changes state, the volume changes. Substances increase in volume when warmed and decrease when cooled.

When a substance changes states, it also changes [ ]. Substances often increase in volume when they are warmed and decrease when cooled. However, water does not follow this rule. When water changes from a solid to a liquid, its volume decreases.

Even as the state of matter changes, the [ ] does not change. Whether the water is warmed or cooled, the number of atoms in it does not increase or decrease.

gas / mass / liquid / evaporates / solid / volume

Complete the exercise.

Math Mission

Look at the table with the results of a study of the length of time water was heated and the temperature of the water. Which is correct when graphing this result?

heating time (minute)	0 min.	3 min.	6 min.	9 min.	12 min.	15 min.	18 min.	21 min.	24 min.	27 min.	30 min.
water temperature (°C)	19°C	35°C	58°C	72°C	85°C	91°C	98°C	99°C	99°C	99°C	99°C

Ans. [ ]

A
B
water temperature (°C)
0 10 20 30 40 50 60 70 80 90 100
3 6 9 12 15 18 21 24 27 30
heating time (minute)

Chapter 8

Changes in States of Matter

Read the mission. Then, answer the following questions to help you with your solution.

The Mission

You are in charge of feeding your baby brother lunch. He's crying for a jam sandwich and won't stop crying until he gets it! But the jam jar is stuck shut! Think of a way to open the sticky jam jar using what you have learned in Chapter 8 to help you solve this problem.

Before you design...THINK!

1. Describe the mission in your own words.

2. Brainstorm your solution. Write your notes in the space below.
   Use the following questions to guide your thinking:

(1) How can you change the properties of the jar to help open the jar?
(2) Can you heat or cool the jar?
(3) What forms of matter are you dealing with? Solids, liquids, or gases? Can you change the properties of one of them to help you?

48 Missions

Chapter 8

Changes in States of Matter

Read the mission. Then, draw and evaluate your solution.

The Mission

You are in charge of feeding your baby brother lunch. He's crying for a jam sandwich and won't stop crying until he gets it! But the jam jar is stuck shut! Think of a way to open the sticky jam jar using what you have learned in Chapter 8 to help you solve this problem.

Design

Draw or write about your solution below.

Evaluate

How did you open the jar? Did you heat it to loosen the lid? Or freeze it so the jar would expand? Do you think your plan would cause the jar to break?

Answer Key Complete STEM Missions Grades 3-5 Earth Science

Chapter 1 Severe Weather

1

Test your knowledge

(1) B (2) C

2

Test your knowledge

(1) C (2) B (3) A (4) D

3

Test your knowledge

(1) T (2) F (3) T

4

Review the Key Points

atmosphere / severe weather / shutters / alert

Math Mission

(1) 30 °F

(2) $110 - 70 = 40$ Ans. 40 °F

(3) $110 - 30 = 80$ Ans. 80 °F

5 (Sample Response)

Before you design... THINK!

1. Create a protection system or device to keep my house safe from bad weather.
2. I think I will improve on the hurricane shutters and figure out how to use tools to warn people about the hurricane.
   Maybe I will use a warning system like a siren in my town or something that is sent to your phone.

6 (Sample Response)

Design

My device would attach to hurricane shutters on people's homes. When the wind blew at a certain speed, the device would make the shutters close over the window. This would help keep people safe.

Evaluate

I think my system will work. I think a problem could be that the wind sensors would close the window with any high winds, not just during a hurricane.

Chapter 2 Beach Erosion

7

Test your knowledge

(1) weathering

(2) erosion

(3) people

8

Test your knowledge

(1) F (2) T (3) F

9

Test your knowledge

(1) C (2) B (3) A

10

Review the Key Points

Weathering / Erosion / beach sand / Strong winds

Math Mission

(1) $2 \times 10 = 20$ Ans. 20 feet

(2) $36 \div 6 = 6$ Ans. 6 years

(3) $24 \div 4 = 6$ Ans. 6 trucks

11 (Sample Response)

Before you design... THINK!

1. Create a plan to help save the beach from further erosion and to restore it.
2. - bring more sand to the beach as a start
   - create a barrier to keep the sand on the beach and not let it be washed away
   - mesh netting? - use a semi-solid barrier that lets water through, but not sand

12 (Sample Response)

Design

I would build a mesh barrier that was designed to keep sand on the beach but let water through. It would be attached to ropes on the shore and people could pull it in to bring back the sand that washed away.

Evaluate

My design could be improved by finding a natural way to help stop beach erosion instead of adding manmade objects to the beach.

Chapter 3 Tectonic Plates

13

Test your knowledge

(1) A (2) C

14

Test your knowledge

(1) C (2) B (3) D

15

Test your knowledge

(1) B (2) A

16

Review the Key Points

mantle / Tectonic plates / earthquake / epicenter / seismograph

Math Mission

(1) 1000 (2) A (3) C

17 (Sample Response)

Before you design... THINK!

1. Design a device or plan to help earthquake proof buildings.
2. I could improve existing technology to help make homes safer.
   One existing technology I could improve on is what material buildings are made of. Plastic is a flexible and sturdy material I could use in my design.

18 (Sample Response)

Design

I would design a way to build part of my structure out of strong and flexible plastic that would bend and move as the earthquake shook the building. It would have flexible plastic joints that connected strong metal beams. The metal beams would hold up the structure and the plastic joints would help it bend.

Evaluate

I think my design would work because it would make the structure more resistant to the earthquake's shock waves. I think one issue would be that it would be hard to test and make sure my idea works to keep a building safe during a real earthquake.

Chapter 4 Flooding

Test your knowledge

B

Test your knowledge

Test your knowledge

Review the Key Points

flood / heavy rain / floodplain / dikes

Math Mission

(1) A

(2) $100 \times 3 = 300$ Ans. 300 m

(3) $500 \div 100 = 5$ Ans. 5 cm

23 (Sample Response)

Before you design... THINK!

1. Create a plan to keep people safe from floods or stop flooding from damaging the community.
2. - build something to help prevent a flood
   - stop rising water from overflowing the river bank
   - design something to divert flood waters

24 (Sample Response)

Design

For this mission, I would improve on existing flood barriers. I would build a levee to prevent water from reaching the town, but it would have some slides or chutes coming down from the top that collected the over-flowing water and directed it to a smaller reservoir away from the town. The flood water could then be used by the people in the town for energy or farming.

Evaluate

I think my design could work as long as the overflow water went into the chutes and did not overflow past them. It would not work as well during a flash flood.

Chapter 5 Changing Climates

25

Test your knowledge

(1) F (2) T (3) F

26

Test your knowledge

(1) D (2) C (3) A (4) B

27

Test your knowledge

(1) T (2) F (3) T

28

Review the Key Points

Climate / sea level / Global warming / greenhouse effect

Math Mission

(1) $3 \times 5 = 15$ Ans. 15 minutes

(2) $60 \div 3 = 20$ Ans. 20 saplings

(3) $30 \div 3 = 10$

10 (number of saplings for one adult can plant in 30 minutes) × 3 (number of adults) = 30

Ans. 30 saplings

29 (Sample Response)

Before you design... THINK!

1. Create a plan to inform people about changing climates.
2. I would need to do more research on how changing climates affect the world around me and my community. I could create a monthly newsletter and send it to all of my community in the mail or by email.

30 (Sample Response)

Design

My plan to inform my community about changing climates would be to create a monthly newsletter that I could send by email or mail to help inform people about it. The newsletter would explain what is happening and tell people ways to help.

Evaluate

I think my newsletter would be successful in informing people in my community about the dangers of the changing climate. I think it may be hard to get people to read it or sign up to get it, but once they do I think it will help.

Chapter 6 Landslides

31

Test your knowledge

(1) T (2) F (3) T

32

Test your knowledge

A, C, D

33

Test your knowledge

B

34

Review the Key Points

landslide / slopes / gravity / monitor / evacuation

Math Mission

(1) 200 mm (2) 150 mm (3) 400 mm (4) A

35 (Sample Response)

Before you design... THINK!

1. Create a piece of technology or plan to help prevent landslides from damaging a community.
2. I will use current technology to create my protection system and keep people and the town safe from landslides.
   I will use materials that are flexible, so if they are hit by a landslide they bounce back.
   I will also create an escape plan to help people get to safety.

36 (Sample Response)

Design

My plan would be to create flexible sensors that could be put in holes in the hillside to help measure the land sliding. They would be flexible plastic or rubber so they could move with the ground and alert scientists if the ground slides too much. The scientists can read the measurements and help determine if a landslide could happen there.

Evaluate

I think one issue would be if the sensors aren't dug deep enough into the hillside they could be in the landslide.

Chapter 7 Natural Resources for Energy

37

Test your knowledge

(1) A (2) C

38

Test your knowledge

(1) T (2) T (3) F

39

Test your knowledge

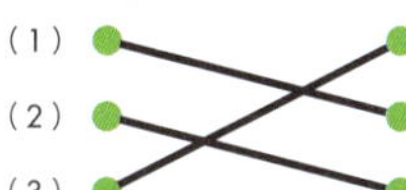

40

Review the Key Points

natural / energy / oil / original / renewable

Math Mission

(1) $100 \times 8 = 800$ Ans. 800 kW

(2) $4500 \div 1500 = 3$ Ans. 3 windmills

41 (Sample Response)

Before you design... THINK!

1. Create a renewable energy plan for your town.
2. Figure out what type of renewable energy to use in the plan.
   Where I live is really sunny, so I will use solar energy.
   How can I distribute my plan in my community?

42 (Sample Response)

Design

Create a solar panel field that the whole town can access power from, to help people use renewable energy.

Evaluate

Some people in the community might not want to be part of the plan. They may be more concerned with what it will cost to build than with how it will help.

Chapter 8 Disposing of Waste

43

Test your knowledge

A, C, D

44

Test your knowledge

(1) C (2) A (3) B

45

Test your knowledge

(1) A (2) C

46

Review the Key Points

waste / biodegradable / Burying / Landfills

Math Mission

(1) 3-6 months

(2) 2-4 weeks

(3) aluminum soda can

47 (Sample Response)

Before you design... THINK!

1. Create a better way to get rid of waste.
2. Some problems with modern landfills are leaks and dangerous chemicals.
   My design will address these issues with better materials.
   Create a plan that offers people an incentive for recycling or composting.
   Can we encourage people to make less waste?

48 (Sample Response)

Design

Create a conveyer belt that will sort the garbage so less waste ends up in landfills. This will help landfill have less waste. Add a second layer of material that will absorb any of the liquid waste that tries to leak through the plastic lining. It will help stop leaks from getting into the dirt and ground water.

Evaluate

I think my technology will help less trash go to the landfill, because recyclable and compost material will not end up in the landfill and can get reused. Then, my absorbing layer will help keep the land around the landfill safe from the material that is thrown away.

Answer Key

Complete STEM Missions Grades 3-5 Life Science

Chapter 1 Plant Adaptations

1

Test your knowledge

(1) C (2) B

2

Test your knowledge

(1) C (2) A (3) B

3

Test your knowledge

(1) B (3) A (5) A
(2) C (4) B (6) D

4

Review the Key Points

adaptation / environment / seeds / animals

Math Mission

(1) 50 mm (2) A (3) B

5 (Sample Response)

Before you design... THINK!

1. Create a new type of seed that will travel far, so it can find a good place to grow.
2. My seed would use an exploding seed pod and smooth seed shape to sail through the air and land farther away from the parent plant. It would grow in a field like environment, so good soil is nearby.

6 (Sample Response)

Design

My seed would explode from a seed pod. It would be streamline and smooth, like an arrowhead. So it would sail through the air further from the parent plant.

Evaluate

My seed looks like a sunflower's seed, but animals cannot eat it. So it needs to explode from the pod and fly through the air. As long as it finds good soil it will grow.

Chapter 2 Pollination

7

Test your knowledge

(1) A (2) B

8

Test your knowledge

(1) C (2) D

9

Test your knowledge

10

Review the Key Points

Pollination / pollinator / pollen

Math Mission

(1) $25 \times 10 = 250$ Ans. 250 flowers
(2) $1000 \times 5 = 5000$ Ans. 5000 flowers
(3) $12 \div 4 = 3 \quad 2 \times 3 = 6$ Ans. 6 hours

11 (Sample Response)

Before you design... THINK!

1. Create a tool to help farmers pollinate more flowers on their apple trees.
2. Bees are good pollinators because they have tiny hairs on their bodies that collect and hold pollen. They can also fly from one flower to another, which helps cross-pollinate many flowers.
   Other traits from pollinators that could be helpful would be the shape of their mouths or body parts that collect the pollen. Like a hummingbird's beak helps it get food and pollen from long tube like flowers.

12 (Sample Response)

Design

- Use a stick with pipe cleaners attached. They can be bent in different ways to reflect different types of flowers / pollinaters.
- The bristles will mimic the hair on bee's legs.

Evaluate

One part of my device that could be improved is how the pollen is removed from the bristles. With this device the farmer has to shake the stick over the flowers to get the pollen off. I think there could be a better method.

Chapter 3 Animal Adaptations

Test your knowledge

Test your knowledge

A → E → B → D → C

Test your knowledge

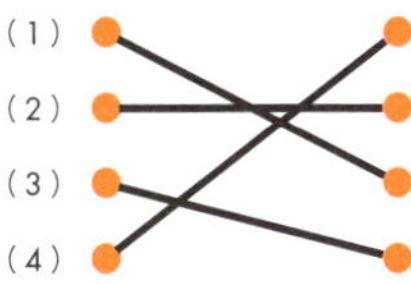

16

Review the Key Points

adaptations / food / child / beaks

Math Mission

(1) 4 (2) 10 (3) spoon

17 (Sample Response)

Before you design... THINK!

1. Create an animal that could live in the cave environment.
2. The weather might be warm during the day and cold at night because the cave is dark.
   Small plants would grow here because it is dark and only gets a little sunlight.
   Being able to see in the dark would be useful to animals who live in this type of environment.

18 (Sample Response)

Design

My animal would have big eyes so it could see better in the low light of the cave. It would have a sticky tongue like a frog to help it catch the bugs and lizards that live in the cave too. My animal would have wide paddle-like feet like a duck to help it walk on the muddy ground.

Evaluate

I think my animal could be better adapted to surviving in the wet cave environment if it had thick fur to keep it warm. An adaptation that would not help my animal would be sharp claws on its feet because they would sink into the mud.

Chapter 4 Habitat Change

19

Test your knowledge

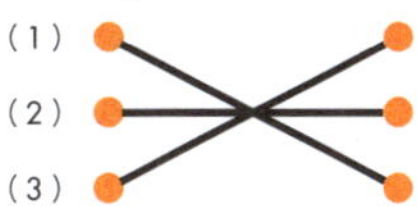

20

Test your knowledge

(1) D (2) B

21

Test your knowledge

D

22

Review the Key Points

habitat / adapt / extinct / People / corridors

Math Mission

(1) $4 \times 3 = 12$ Ans. 12 km^2

(2) $(4 + 12) \times 2 = 32$ Ans. 32 km^2

(3) $32 \div 2 = 16$ Ans. 16 km^2

23 (Sample Response)

Before you design... THINK!

1. Build a school building that is safe for animals and people.
2. I could build my school building off the side of a mountain or hill. I would make sure that it would not bother the trees growing there. My building would be built around trees, so no land has to change.

24 (Sample Response)

Design

Instead of leveling a hill side to build on flat ground, we can build a platform off the side to support the school not change the landscape.

Evaluate

One challenge is it would take a lot of resources to build the platform to support a whole building. The land would still be changed by the supports.

Chapter 5 Invasive Species

25

Test your knowledge

B

26

Test your knowledge

(1) C (2) B (3) A

27

Test your knowledge

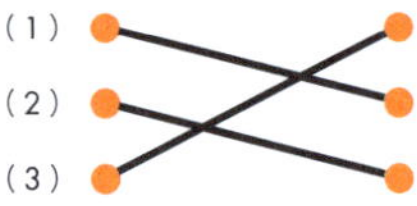

28

Review the Key Points

invasive / pets / native / resources / live

Math Mission

(1) 17 feet (2) 15 days

29 (Sample Response)

Before you design... THINK!

1. Create a plan to help stop invasive animals or plants from finding their way to new places.
2. I think I will focus on zebra mussels and how to stop them from moving to new bodies of water.
   Since they spread using boats, I will find a way to stop them from getting on the boats in the first place.

30 (Sample Response)

Design

- Create a spray for the hull of boats that is slippery and doesn't allow the mussels to attach to the boats.
- This will help stop people from bringing them by boat to other waterways.

Evaluate

What could be improved is how to get people to use the spray. Can it be made mandatory for people use? We would also have to make the spray safe for the environment so it doesn't cause more problems.

Chapter 6 Germs

31

Test your knowledge

(1) B (2) D

32

Test your knowledge

(1) F (2) F (3) T

33

Test your knowledge

(1) C (2) D (3) B (4) A

34

Review the Key Points

germs / Bacteria / Viruses / diseases

Math Mission

(1) 100 (2) 400 (3) 120 minutes

35 (Sample Response)

Before you design... THINK!

1. Create a way to kill germs, or prevent them from spreading, that is safe for people.
2. Some ways to kill germs are: UV light, super hot steam, or chemicals.
   We can also stop germs from spreading by washing our hands with soap and water.
   Soap and water is safe for people to use to get rid of germs.

36 (Sample Response)

Design

- Stand on UV lightbulbs for 1 minute.
- Kill germs on shoes.

Evaluate

One challenge would be that UV light can be harmful to humans, the device would have to only shine light on the person's shoes.

Chapter 7 How Plants Grow

37

Test your knowledge

(1) A, B, D (2) C

38

Test your knowledge

B

39

Test your knowledge

(1) B (2) B (3) A → C → B → D

40

Review the Key Points

water / carbon dioxide / photosynthesis / oxygen

Math Mission

(1) 12 hours (2) 20 minutes (3) B

41 (Sample Response)

Before you design... THINK!

1. Create a plan for growing plants without soil on a spaceship.
2. Plants need water, nutrients, carbon dioxide, and sunlight to grow.
   People produce carbon dioxide so we would not need to bring it with us. People also need water to drink so we would have to bring a lot of water for people and to grow plants.
   We would also need to make sunlight and provide the nutrients for the plants.

42 (Sample Response)

Design

- Rotating wheel so plants get equal sunlight and carbon dioxide as they move.
- Create a light bulb that acts as artificial sunlight to provide the plants with sun.
- Use recycled water from people cooking and cleaning on the spaceship to water the plants.

Evaluate

The method could grow a lot of food. However it would be hard to bring all the liquid nutrients to feed the plants.

Chapter 8 Decomposition

43

Test your knowledge

(1) D (2) C

44

Test your knowledge

(1) A (2) C (3) B

45

Test your knowledge

A

46

Review the Key Points

decomposition / fungi / bacteria / compost

Math Mission

(1) 4000 gallons
(2) 1200 gallons
(3) 3600 gallons

47 (Sample Response)

Before you design... THINK!

1. Create a plan to make people compost more.
2. The steps for composting are compiling the waste materials, adding a decomposer, and making sure the compost has a safe place to decay.
   I could use worms as decomposers.
   Some people might not like compost in their homes because it is smelly. Other people might not have the space for it.

48 (Sample Response)

Design

- Create a town incentive program for bringing waste materials to a local compost site.
- Offer rewards for every bag of food scrapes saved and composted. For example, if people bring a pound of food scraps to add to the compost they can take home fruit and vegetables grown in the compost garden.

Evaluate

This would be a good system, but it would take time to get people to use it. It would also cost a lot to reward people for participating.

Complete STEM Missions Grades 3-5

Answer Key

Physical Science

Chapter 1 Forces and Motion

Test your knowledge

(1) B (2) A

2

Test your knowledge

(1) balanced (2) balanced (3) unbalanced

3

Test your knowledge

(1) B (2) A

4

Review the Key Points

force / Direction / balanced / unbalanced / Friction

Math Mission

(1) $8\frac{1}{2}$ cm (8.5 cm) (3) 3 cm

(2) 5 cm (4) tile floor

5 (Sample Response)

Before you design... THINK!

1. Use knowledge of forces to build the fastest sled and win the race.
2. I could make my sled legs out of metal so it glides on the icy parts and the top part out of wood so it weighs less.

6 (Sample Response)

Design

- My sled legs would be made of metal like an ice skate blade to go fast on the icy parts of the hill.
- I would build the top part of my sled out of wood so it was lighter. This can help it go faster too.

Evaluate

My sled would win the race! If I had to change part of my design, I would find a way to make my sled more slippery so it creates less friction.

Chapter 2 Simple Machines

Test your knowledge

(1) force (2) done (3) not done

8

Test your knowledge

(1) B (2) C (3) A

9

Test your knowledge

(1) inclined plane (2) wedge (3) screw

10

Review the Key Points

Work / simple / lever / wedge / compound

Math Mission

(1) $10 \div 2 = 5$ $30 \div 5 = 6$ Ans. 6 pounds

(2) $8 \div 4 = 2$ $40 \div 2 = 20$ Ans. 20 pounds

11 (Sample Response)

Before you design... THINK!

1. Find a way to open the chest you found with the help of simple machines.
2. I could use a lever and a pulley to open the chest. I don't think a screw would be helpful.

12 (Sample Response)

Design

Use a wedge to try the chest open, then use a pulley to help lift the heavy lid.

Evaluate

I used a wedge and a pulley to open the chest. I could've used a lever to help open the chest. It could've made it easier.

Chapter 3 Magnets

13

Test your knowledge

B, D, E

14

Test your knowledge

(1) repel (2) attract (3) attract (4) repel

15

Test your knowledge

A, B, C, D, E, F, G, H (all)

16

Review the Key Points

magnetic field / metals / north pole / Magnets

Math Mission

(1) Yes (2) No

17 (Sample Response)

Before you design... THINK!

1. Create a device to help pick up all the pins quickly and without getting hurt.
2. I would use multiple magnets for this plan. By using more magnets, I can pick up more pins at once.

18 (Sample Response)

Design

Glue magnets to the end of a rake or several sticks to move over the rug and collect the pins.

Evaluate

I think my tool would pick up most of the pins easily. I think I would need to add something to the tool to help make sure all the pins are picked up, like the screen on a metal detector.

Chapter 4 Forms of Energy

19

Test your knowledge

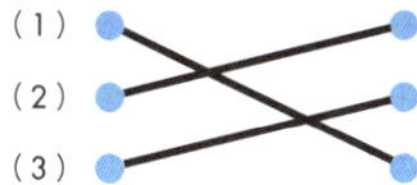

20

Test your knowledge

A, B, D

21

Test your knowledge

(1) T (3) F (5) T
(2) F (4) T

22

Review the Key Points

energy conversion / temperature / insulator / opaque / reflection

Math Mission

(1) 100 – 75 = 25 Ans. 25 degrees
(2) 80 – 65 = 15 Ans. 15 degrees
(3) 108 – 60 = 48 Ans. 48 degrees

23 (Sample Response)

Before you design... THINK!

1. Create a way to keep your small house warm with energy.
2. I would build my house out of material that conducts heat well so it stays in the room.

24 (Sample Response)

Design

- Metal is a good conductor, so I would build the outside of the house out of metal to help conduct heat and keep the house warm.
- I would put big windows in the walls and roof to help bring in more light for the metal walls to absorb.

Evaluate

I would need to use specific conductors and insulators to make my solution work. I'm not sure how I would light the room when it is not sunny.

Chapter 5 Electricity

25

Test your knowledge

(1) B (2) A (3) C (4) C

26

Test your knowledge

(1) F (2) T (3) T

27

Test your knowledge

A, B, C, D (all)

28

Review the Key Points

circuit / conductor / batteries / series / parallel / charging

Math Mission

(1) 18 – 7 = 11 Ans. 11 hours
(2) 40 – 2 = 38 Ans. 38 hours

29 (Sample Response)

Before you design... THINK!

1. Create a plan to fix the broken light circuit in the house.
2. I can use parallel circuits and more batteries to help fix the light issues.

30 (Sample Response)

Design

Use the symbols from the circuit map to plan a better circuit layout for the light bulbs in the house. Make sure there are enough batteries to support all the lights.

Evaluate

I think my plan will help the lights work better in the house.

Chapter 6 Sound Waves

31

Test your knowledge

(1) T (2) T (3) F (3) F

32

Test your knowledge

(1) C (2) C (3) B

33

Test your knowledge

(1) B (2) D (3) C (4) A

34

Review the Key Points

vibrates / sound waves / pitch / frequency / volume / resonance

Math Mission

(1) $340 \times 2 = 680$ Ans. 680 m
(2) $340 \times 5 = 1700$ Ans. 1700 m

35 (Sample Response)

Before you design... THINK!

1. Create an original instrument that can make lots of types of sounds.
2. I could use hard materials to make sounds louder or soft materials to make lower sounds.

36 (Sample Response)

Design

- My instrument is like a drum, but you can take the center piece out to make the sound louder or softer. The piece is made of cloth that will make the sound softer.
- If the piece is removed it allows for the sound to echo and be louder.

Evaluate

I think my instrument was successful in making different types of sounds. I could improve my instrument by creating more ways to make it sound louder.

Chapter 7 Structures of Matter

Test your knowledge

(1) C (2) A, B, C, D (all)

38

Test your knowledge

(1) T (2) T (3) F

39

Test your knowledge

(1) C (2) B (3) A

40

Review the Key Points

volume / mass / Physical / chemical / atoms / elements

Math Mission

(1) 200 g (2) 800 g (3) 500 g

41 (Sample Response)

Before you design... THINK!

1. Define the properties of the new substance you created.
2. I will give my substance physical and chemical properties. It will have a color, a hardness, and a chemical reaction to rain.

42 (Sample Response)

Design

My substance is called floriandizole. It is purplish in color and harder than diamonds. But it has a chemical property, it can be dissolved in water.

Evaluate

I think my substance would react well with other substances, but it could not be used to build anything outside because rain would melt it.

Chapter 8 Changes in States of Matter

Test your knowledge

(1)
(2)
(3)

Test your knowledge

(1) 100 (3) solid
(2) gas (4) temperature

45

Test your knowledge

(1) increase (2) increase (3) not change

46

Review the Key Points

solid / liquid / gas / evaporates / volume / mass

Math Mission

A

47 (Sample Response)

Before you design... THINK!

1. Find a way to open the stuck jam jar using properties of matter.
2. The jar is stuck closed, but the jam is kind of a liquid. Maybe I could heat or cool it to help open it? Would I need other tools? Like a pot?

48 (Sample Response)

Design

I would put the jam jar in a pot of water and boil it. I would hope that the solid sticky jam on the lid warms up and changes to a liquid jam. This would allow me to open the jar!

Evaluate

I think changing the properties of the jam by heating it would allow me to open it and solve the problem. I think I could have also put the jar in the freezer to see if the jam would expand as it froze and pop the lid off.